What I Have Learned So Far...
And How It Can Help You

From 50 Graduates of the
"School of Hard Knocks"

Paul Bates and Al Emid

WINNIPEG, MANITOBA, CANADA

Paul Bates and Al Emid

WHAT I HAVE LEARNED SO FAR... AND HOW IT CAN HELP YOU
From 50 Graduates of the "School of Hard Knocks"

Printed and bound in Canada

Library and Archives Canada Cataloguing in Publication

Bates, Paul K. (Paul Kevin), 1950-
    What I have learned so far— and how it can help you : clues for succeeding in crisis from 50 graduates of the "School of Hard Knocks" / Paul Bates and Al Emid.

ISBN 978-1-897526-52-1

    1. Success in business. 2. Success. 3. Interviews—Canada.
I. Emid, Al, 1946- II. Title.

HF5386.B2754 2010   650.1   C2010-906911-0

Published by:
Knowledge Bureau, Inc.
187 St. Mary's Road, Winnipeg, Manitoba Canada R2H 1J2
204-953-4769 Email: reception@knowledgebureau.com

Publisher: Evelyn Jacks
Editor: Tessa Wilmott
Cover Design: Don Jacks
Page Design: Sharon Jones

To my grandchildren.

— PAUL BATES

To the individuals who shared their crises and solutions, during both formal interviews and what may have seemed like endless back-checking. In some cases, the interviews caused them personal distress and I thank them for enduring it.

— AL EMID

Also by Paul Bates

Sales Force Management in the Financial Services (2004)

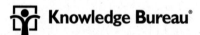 Knowledge Bureau®

Knowledge Bureau Newsbooks are available at special discounts to use as sales promotions or for advisor/corporate training programs. For more information, address a query to

The Knowledge Bureau
reception@knowledgebureau.com
1-866-953-4769
www.knowledgebureau.com

Acknowledgements

Publishing a book is not a solitary effort. There is always a long list of people who helped make it happen. *What I Have Learned So Far and How It Can Help You* is no exception. But our list may be even longer, thanks to the fifty "graduates" of the School of Hard Knocks who shared their stories with us in the hopes that you, the reader, could learn from their experiences. Indeed, when we first asked Terry Jacks to participate in this book, he responded: "Let's try it out. Then, if it can be beneficial to other people, great."

We sincerely thank them for talking to us with honesty and openness. And we thank them for their courage. These were not always easy interviews; many of the individuals relived painful experiences in the retelling. For that, we are humbled and extremely grateful. We can only conclude that our fifty graduates believed in our goal and thank them for travelling with us.

We also thank Ottawa journalist Shannon Lee Mannion, Toronto Media Consultant Suzen Fromstein, Exit Planning Specialist Peter Merrick, CTV's Patrick Foran and several others not mentioned by name. You know who you are. Named and unnamed, these individuals acted as intermediaries in expediting sensitive interviews — essentially lending us the trust that the interviewees had for them. Again, we are most grateful.

Authors customarily thank the publisher and others whose efforts contributed to the realization of their book. And we certainly extend our thanks to publisher Evelyn Jacks, president of The Knowledge Bureau, and her colleague, Donna Lesage, who herded the chapters through to completion. Ditto to Sharon Jones of Typeworks in Winnipeg, the book's designer.

And a final word of thanks to our editor, Tessa Wilmott, and research assistant Sabrina Jeria. We could not have pulled this together without you.

Preface

Someone once said: "Sometimes you have to leave the life you have in order to find the life that is waiting for you."

Like many young men, I was an angry teenager. I grew up in the East End of London, the son of a hard-working and deeply caring couple who managed to make ends meet but never much more. By my early teens, I felt increasing anger at my lot in life and had started down a treacherous path.

One Wednesday, a thoughtful and attentive art teacher asked me to stay after class. He laid out pots of paint and a large sheet of paper. He invited me to stay behind and paint something. I watched him leave, wondering why he was picking on me. Then, I thought, "Why not, I'll give it a try." I began to paint.

It turns out that I could draw, although not well enough to call myself an artist. Yet, it changed my life: I found I could communicate creatively. I began to write and discovered literature. Today, I understand that, of all the skills there are to own, communication is the greatest; communication is the beginning of connection.

What I Have Learned So Far and How It Can Help You is designed to be an intervention for you. It is an opportunity to listen to people whose life stories may be the nudge you need to move in a new direction. We often internalize and cope with dilemma and change by listening to the stories of others. These glimpses into the lives of others allow us to project ourselves into such circumstances, giving us the tools and the confidence we need to move on.

In these stories, you will find ample evidence of the power of the human spirit and its capacity to adapt.

PAUL K. BATES
DECEMBER 2010

Forty-four years of asking questions of people carries with it some advantages, chief among them a continuing awareness of the fragile nature of the relationship between interviewer and interviewee. The interviewer needs valuable information; the interviewee wonders how much information to share yet maintain cherished privacy.

The mission becomes more difficult — and the responsibility more onerous — when writing a book such as *What I have Learned So Far and How It Can Help You*, in which we plumb the personal moments of fifty very worthwhile people. How deeply do you question a woman who is coming to grips with child abuse? How do you pry details from a man whose wife has been diagnosed with cancer?

Yet, they agreed to share their brutal experiences because they appreciated the purpose of this book: that readers might project themselves into the text and find experiences similar to their own — and learn from the solutions employed by our graduates of the School of Hard Knocks.

We set out to provide useful narratives in hopes of telegraphing several concepts, chief among them that most of life's crises have workable solutions. As Andrew Alexander of Second City Inc. says: "Everything is persistence, getting up off the mat and getting back at it. You either get up or you don't."

I hope we have succeeded in what we set out to do. If you know of a story that you believe we should examine for a future edition, please send a note to LearnedSoFar@alemid.com

AL EMID
DECEMBER 2010

Contents

INTRODUCTION

"Prepare for the unknown by studying how others in the past have coped with the unforeseeable and the unpredictable."

— GEORGE S. PATTON

George Patton, the American general who distinguished himself in the North African and Sicilian campaigns of the Second World War, was certainly well acquainted with the unforeseeable and the unpredictable. As military historians will tell you, very few battles go as planned.

The same can be said about life. Very few, if any, lives go as planned. Life is not a straight road. Instead, we are met with strange twists and unexpected turns. And at some point, we all come around a corner and run smack into adversity. Some of us even come eye-to-eye with adversity more than once. So, to take a page from General Patton's book, the best way to prepare for those unexpected and often harsh events is to study how others in the past have coped.

That is the raison d'être of *What I Have Learned So Far and How It Can Help You*. In the following pages, you will meet fifty people. They come from all walks of life, all sectors of society, but they have one thing in common: they have all faced adversity. They have tackled challenges big and small and sometimes downright overwhelming — and they have prevailed.

Some of the names you will recognize, like musician Terry Jacks and comedian Colin Mochrie. Perhaps you'll have read of their exploits in the newspapers, like Crazy Canuck Dave Irwin and Olympic rower Marnie McBean. Some of the people profiled are everyday people who have tackled unusual events with grace and courage, like Gary Reinblatt and Francis McNamara. Some of them stand out because of their deep conviction to a cause, like Justin Cooper. All of them have something to teach you by their example.

By studying how these "graduates" of the School of Hard Knocks have coped with the unforeseeable and the unpredictable, you can prepare yourself for that inevitable bump in the road that could send your life plan careening.

Of course, the circumstances may differ. You may not encounter the exact same problems as the people profiled in *What I Have Learned So Far*. Hopefully, you'll never suffer a brain injury as severe as Dave Irwin has, but hopefully when you do meet adversity big or small, you can meet it with the same determination and optimism that Irwin applied to his recovery. The circumstances may change but the coping skills can be applied in any situation.

As you share the experiences of people in the pages to come, remember: it is not so much the challenge but how you face up to it that counts.

Be careful what you wish for:
How Terry Jacks, Andy Creeggan, Dianne Buckner and Colin Mochrie stayed true to their values, even in the spotlight's glare

"I think that everybody should get rich and famous and do everything they ever dreamed of, so that they can see that it is not the answer."

— TERRY JACKS

Everybody likes a little limelight in their lives — to discover something in themselves that is outstanding. For some, that translates into a career in the public eye, even fame and fortune. But as singer/songwriter Terry Jacks, musician Andrew Creeggan, TV host Dianne Buckner and comedian Colin Mochrie will tell you, standing out can come with its own set of problems. You can find adversity in undreamed of places.

—◁◦▷—

In 1969, you couldn't turn on the radio without hearing *Which Way You Goin' Billy?*. Teenagers sang along with the award-winning hit by The Poppy Family. The single sold 3.5 million records worldwide and topped the charts in Canada and the U.S. It also thrust the husband

and wife team behind The Poppy Family — Terry Jacks, then twenty-five, and Susan Pesklevits, then twenty-two — onto the world stage and into the spotlight.

That was just the beginning of Jacks's rise to stardom. By 1975, Jacks's *Seasons in the Sun* had won him a number of awards, including Male Vocalist of the Year in both 1974 and 1975 and Best-Selling Single in 1974 and 1975. The song, inspired by a young friend dying of leukemia and produced and partially written by Jacks, remains the biggest-selling single internationally by a Canadian artist, tallying almost fourteen million copies sold.

Ironically, the height of Jacks's fame was also the depth of his disillusionment. His marriage to Pesklevits had ended after five-and-a-half years and he was on his own. The strain of writing, producing and touring was taking its toll. "I got *there*," he says, "and that's where you're on top and you're rich and famous. You have everything you want — and you find that that's not the answer."

Jacks set out to find that answer.

As a teenager in Vancouver, Winnipeg-born Jacks dreamt of music not as records but as "little stories" he could tell. He spent the money he earned on his paper route on popular recordings, such as *The Story of My Life* by Marty Robbins. Like other teenaged boys at the time, he slicked his hair back with Brylcreem and practised in front of a mirror with a guitar. "It only had a couple of strings," he says of his guitar. "I pretended I was Buddy Holly."

He started writing songs and formed a surfing band. But it wasn't until 1963, when he and a friend started a group called The Chessmen that he gained some recognition. The Chessmen played local clubs until 1966. About that time, Jacks met Pesklevits, a vocalist from Saskatoon, Saskatchewan.

Jacks loved Pesklevits's voice. "It was real," he recalls four decades after their first encounter. "She was singing from her heart."

They married and formed The Poppy Family. The rest is Canadian music history.

But Jacks was never comfortable with fame. He didn't like touring or media appearances. He preferred producing to performing. And the conviction that some of his work had been wrongfully copied led him to set up his own publishing company. "I learned that in this business there were a lot of crooks," he says.

As he turned his back on fame, Jacks began his search for a more fulfilling personal philosophy. "So, I looked for the answer," he says. "I could do anything I wanted. I travelled like mad, did whatever I wanted."

He became interested in environmental issues, a dedication that eventually won him the United Nations Association Western Canada Wilderness Environmental Award in 1992. "I saw the destruction on the British Columbia coast from the pulp mills. It was the most toxic industry in North America pumping toxic compounds into our atmosphere and our water every day," he says. "So, I looked into that and found that none of the pulp mills were following their permits." He also found government agencies that failed to enforce environmental laws.

But Jacks didn't find the answer and the peace he was looking for until 1989, when he bought his first Bible. He had become interested in the teachings of Robert Schuller, Sr., on the television program *Hour of Power*. Schuller's message was different from the one Jacks was used to. "I always thought that Christianity was doom and gloom," Jacks says. "Schuller had such a positive approach to everything. I knew that I had this hole inside me and I didn't know what it was. I prayed for understanding of the Bible and that began to fill this void within me."

Yet, Jacks does not consider himself a "religious" man and, with the exception of the hymns he writes, disavows preaching his beliefs to others. Instead, he takes solace in a philosophy and a way of life that speaks to his individual needs. "I have peace now," he says. "Even when turmoil happens, I have this peace within me."

He views his relationship with Jesus Christ as all-important to his life. "You may never really realize how much you need Him," he says, "until one morning you wake and find that He is all you have."

If you ask Jacks to name the highlights of his life, he lists *Seasons in the Sun*; the 1985 birth of his daughter, Holly (named for Buddy Holly); his United Nations environmental award; and, most important, his realization "the way of Jesus is the only way."

"I think that everybody should get rich and famous and do everything they ever dreamed of," he says, "so that they can see that it's not the answer."

—◁◦▷—

Andy Creeggan, like Jacks, turned his back on fame — and fortune — but not because he was searching for an answer. He already knew what he wanted to be, the life he wanted to live — he just had to find the courage to define success in his own terms, and then live that life.

Creeggan was an early member of Canadian alternative rock band, Barenaked Ladies. Scarborough, Ontario, high-school friends Ed Robertson and Steven Page formed Barenaked Ladies on Oct. 1, 1988, to play a Toronto gig. As the band's popularity grew and the number of gigs increased, Page and Robertson recruited drummer Creeggan, then eighteen, and his brother Jim on bass in December 1989.

Creeggan played with the Ladies for six months, before he joined the Canada World Youth, an international exchange program that took him first to Cowansville, Quebec, in July and to Uruguay in November. That experience left him with a feeling of idealism and a sense of wanting to be "just a regular person."

On his return in 1991, he rejoined Barenaked Ladies, this time on keyboards. In his absence, Tyler Stewart had become the band's drummer. "The band had taken on a real rhythm of its own," says Creeggan. "It was really going somewhere."

He was happy to go along for the ride. He realized that he could contribute to the group, learn something along the way and enjoy a musical bond with other talented musicians. "I was getting a lot out of it," he admits. "But I realized, in the long term, it wasn't necessarily something that I was looking for."

Creeggan had other goals he wanted to pursue. He wanted to get a university education. "That was gradually eating away at me," he says. "I felt like I was a slightly uneducated guy out in the world before he was ready for it."

He also wanted to be a professional percussionist, and indulge his taste for instruments such as the dulcimer. Being on the road with Barenaked Ladies meant that Creeggan could follow his own musical tastes only in his spare time. "Gradually, I realized that touring and being in this band — being a support member of this group — was taking up too much of my time," he says. "I wanted to do other things."

Creeggan also knew there was a lifestyle factor. Instead of fame, he wanted what he describes as a "more grass roots kind of life."

In 1995, Creeggan reached a tipping point. After enjoying a break from touring, the band was in the studio working on its second record album. Creeggan realized that Barenaked Ladies' second album was more than just a follow-on to the first. There was pressure to build on the success of the first; that triggered stress within the group. Creeggan ended up getting sick — twice.

"The body tells you something," he says.

Several hallucinations during his illness revolved around leaving the band. But, still, Creeggan postponed leaving — until after the second album was complete, and the next road tour was over. But this time he kept his promise to himself and, when the time came, he announced his departure.

"It was a very intense time to break it," he admits. "It is hard for a group to continue with confidence when someone has ditched it."

It also had an emotional impact on Creeggan. "There was a sense of relief," he says, "and a slight amount of panic because there is a certain amount of financial protection when you're in a group like that.

"The band structured my life," he adds. "I suddenly had to make a lot more decisions than I ever remembered having to do."

But the knowledge that it was the right thing for him, that it had been coming for a long time, fortified Creeggan's resolve. "I was free to be myself," he says.

So, in 1996, he enrolled in the music composition program at McGill University in Montreal, graduating with a bachelor's degree in 2001. He has continued to perform with his brother Jim as the Brothers Creeggan, something they had started when he was still with the Barenaked Ladies. The Brothers have now recorded four albums and Creeggan has his own project, Andiwork, which allows him to explore the instrumental compositions he likes.

Although he recognizes that he may have been better off financially had he remained with the Barenaked Ladies, he would not have been better off emotionally. "If you measure in dollars, maybe leaving was the wrong thing," he says. "But if you measure it in terms of knowing me and knowing that I've been able to give time to my composing and my kids, and play sports, which is one of my big passions, then it was the right thing."

Defining and measuring success, Creeggan maintains, is up to each individual. You have to identify the things that are important to you, he advises. He did — and it has brought him happiness.

—◁o▷—

Over the course of her career, Dianne Buckner has become comfortable with the high profile her performance as a journalist has earned her. As host of *Dragons' Den*, Canadian Broadcasting Corp.'s hit TV reality show, in which entrepreneurs pitch their business ideas to five self-made millionaires, she tackles her role with assurance. But that wasn't always the case.

In the mid-1980s, when her career accelerated at a faster speed than she had anticipated, she didn't have the same level of confidence in her abilities as she does now. Struggling to meet the rising expectations of her bosses only exacerbated the stress of an already high-stress job. Buckner had to find a way to cope.

Toronto-born Buckner set her sights on a career before the television cameras in the early 1980s. She attended Toronto's Ryerson University and, after she graduated with a B.A. in journalism, landed a job as a junior researcher at CBC. Her first big break came in 1986, when she got the chance to co-host the CTV Television Network's consumer show *Live It Up*. "We were testing products all the time and putting the results on the air," says Buckner. "Sometimes, companies didn't like it."

While at *Live It Up*, Buckner was part of the Toronto Bureau of CTV News and occasionally filled in as a reporter for the network's National News. So, when CTV decided that the popular show had run its course, cancelling it in 1990, she jumped at the opportunity to become a full-time reporter for CTV National News. That summer, she covered the Oka crisis, the confrontation between the Mohawks of the Kanesatake reserve and the town of Oka, Quebec, backed by the Quebec provincial police and eventually the Canadian Forces. Her handling of that story — which dominated headlines from July 11 to September 26 — solidified her reputation and led to more high-profile assignments. Three months later, she got another "big" news assignment, covering the one-year anniversary of the massacre of fourteen young women at Montreal's École Polytechnique.

On December 6, 1989, twenty-five-year-old Marc Lépine gunned down twenty-eight people at the École Polytechnique — twenty-four of them women — before he turned the gun on himself. He blamed "feminism," and the fact that he targeted women imbued the already emotionally charged event with nasty and controversial political overtones.

So, the big news story was also a big stress story for Buckner. She had been at the National News for only six months, yet she was working alone on a major national story, without a producer or a researcher. "That was the key thing," she recalls. "It was a big story; I was on my own. I didn't really have the experience to do it justice."

It affected her eating and sleeping patterns, she admits, and as the deadline approached and stress levels mounted, it got the better of her. In a parking garage, when her foot shifted from the brake pedal to the gas pedal, she ploughed her car into a concrete pillar, injuring her ankle, knee and finger and wrecking the car.

A helpful passerby called an ambulance. "There was a line-up of cars behind me," Buckner recalls. "They couldn't get into the garage because there was a crashed car at the bottom of the ramp and a bloodied woman staggering out of her vehicle."

She spent five days in hospital recovering.

"I should have been more upfront and said, 'I'm not ready for this; this is too much for me. I need help.' That's all I really needed to say," she says, acknowledging that it is not unusual to ask for help on such an assignment. "I'm sure they would have been perfectly happy to do that."

Buckner has not been afraid to ask for help since. In fact, she has become something of an expert on people asking for help and handling stress. As host of *Dragons' Den* and during a ten-year-long stint as host of CBC's *Venture*, she has witnessed on ongoing array of entrepreneurs deal with stress and rejection head on as they battle for the survival of their businesses. In the public forum of a TV reality show, rejection isn't very often pretty. Some contestants cope better than others.

"It's a very specialized thing that the *Dragons' Den* principals are looking for," Buckner says. They are venture capitalists who expect healthy returns on their investments. "They want to see a business that has the potential to grow exponentially."

Many entrepreneurs take the rejection in stride and look elsewhere for the money they need. "It doesn't mean it's the end of the road for them," she says. If they have credible ideas, they look for investors who have different priorities.

For others, rejection necessitates setting aside the disappointment and realistically evaluating the criticisms and reasons for the rejection. What are the strengths, weaknesses, opportunities and threats — "SWOT" analysis — of the business idea? "How tough is the competition? How many products or services out there are like mine? What is my distinguishing benefit?" she asks. Such self-examination can be stressful, but in the end it can also prove profitable.

"It's not the end of the world to say you need help," Buckner argues; it does not amount to an admission of defeat. Now, she whole-heartedly buys into the belief that a wise person knows what he or she does not know, and a strong person knows his or her weaknesses. "That's now my philosophy," she says. "There's no shame in having weaknesses because — guess what? — everybody has them."

—◄○►—

Laughing along with comedian Colin Mochrie is a national pastime. Whether it is TV programs such as *Whose Line Is It Anyway?* or *The Drew Carey Show* or live improv performances, audiences around the world have giggled and guffawed with Mochrie. He has a list of stage, television and movie credits an arm long and awards to match. No wonder he is so good-humoured.

"It has always been a constant shock to me," says the genuine and modest Mochrie, "that I actually make a living from doing something that I love doing."

But Mochrie, too, has had his challenges. Life hasn't always gone as planned; he has been bitten on the backside by reality and made to swallow the bitter pill of disappointment. So, what do you do with shattered dreams? Mochrie will tell you: you dream new ones.

Scotland-born Mochrie got his big break in 1990 at age thirty-four, when the alumnus of comedy theatre Second City landed a role in the British television improv series, *Whose Line Is It Anyway?*. He and his wife, comedian Deborah McGrath, moved to Los Angeles, where she was writing for the television series *My Talk Show*, which she co-created. The Canadian couple were on their way to the big time in the U.S.

Two years later, however, everything had changed. In 1992, *My Talk Show* was cancelled, their son had just been born, the Rodney King riots shook Los Angeles and, although Mochrie continued to be involved with *Whose Line Is It Anyway?*, there was not a lot of other work. Their stash of cash steadily declined and they were falling on hard times. "It seemed every day we were a day closer to being on the street," Mochrie recalls ruefully. "The brutal thing was having no money, no prospects, a young baby and trying to figure out what to do."

Mochrie and McGrath decided to move back to Canada. It wasn't an easy decision and involved seriously taking stock of their talents and their priorities. It called for a brutally honest self-assessment as they decided if chasing the American dream was what they wanted to do. "My advice," says Mochrie, "take a look at your life and see what your priorities are."

In retrospect, returning to Toronto proved to be a wise decision. There were more opportunities open to Mochrie. He started directing the Second City touring company and worked in a musical version of *The Brady Bunch* and the game-show spoof *Supertown Challenge*. He starred in commercials, including the trademark roles of Detergent Crusader for Sunlight Detergent and the Snack Fairy for Nabisco Brands.

In 1995, he landed the role of sidekick Eugene on *The Drew Carey Show*. Since then, he has had regular roles in the 2000-2001 Global Television comedy series *Blackfly*, the Canadian Broadcasting Corp.'s *This Hour Has 22 Minutes*, the CBC's *Getting Along Famously*, and countless guest appearances. Most recently, he has acted in Vision TV's *She's The Mayor*, the first thirteen episodes of which are scheduled to be aired early in 2011.

And, of course, he remained a regular on the British *Whose Line Is It Anyway?* until 1998, when the program ended. But by then, the U.S. had picked up on the idea and Mochrie became a regular on the American version of *Whose Line Is It Anyway?* until 2004, when it ended.

Mochrie still encounters fans who remember how the laughter and silliness of *Whose Line Is It Anyway?* gave them a respite from their own traumas. "People will come up and say, 'You know, I was going through a tough divorce,' or 'My father was dying and for that half hour there was nothing else in the world except laughing,'" he explains. "I've met a psychiatrist who said after 9/11 she recommended to all her patients to watch *Who's Line*, just to forget about everything."

Despite setbacks and having what he refers to as only "one marketable skill," Mochrie has had a productive career. He acknowledges the part luck has played in his success but he also attributes his success to being true to his values and priorities, even in the face of adversity and disappointment. He has always found strength in his personal life and, during that tough time in Los Angeles, took comfort in a marriage that proved strong enough to withstand the financial stresses.

"Financial difficulties can put a lot of strain on a marriage," Mochrie says. "But we never had that. We stuck together as a family."

"Work comes and goes," he adds. "If all you have is work, it stops you from experiencing life and, in my case, life is such a part of work," he says, explaining that his improvisational work is based on observations of people around him. "Have your *life* life as big as your work life. You want to keep your family there at all times."

LEARNED SO FAR

- Live life consistent with your values; don't try to be what you are not.
- There is always a price to be paid for the choices you make.
- Never be afraid to ask for help.
- Maintain balance between your work life and your *life* life.
- Define "success" according to your own terms.

CHAPTER TWO

It takes more than technique to win:
Life lessons Marnie McBean and Mario Lechowski learned from sports

"Just because you're good at what you do doesn't mean that people are going to want to be on a team with you."

— MARNIE McBEAN

Recent research has confirmed something Olympic rower Marnie McBean and boxing champion Mario Lechowski already knew instinctively. Participating in sports prepares you for life. It can boost self-esteem, instill mental toughness and make you better able to cope with the wins and losses of life.

And, as McBean found out, it isn't just the technical skills that make you a champion. It is when the "soft," people skills are added that true winners are created.

◄o►

Olympic champion Marnie McBean has made a great contribution to the sport of rowing and to Canada's place in it. She and rowing partner Kathleen Heddle twice won gold medals for Canada in the Pair events in the Summer Olympics, first in Barcelona in 1992, then in Atlanta in 1996. McBean and Heddle were also part of the teams that won gold in the Eight-oared event in Barcelona and bronze in the Quadruple in Atlanta. In between, McBean won the World Cup in the Single scull in 1994, while she and Heddle won a silver medal in the Double at the World Championships that year. In the next year's World Championships, she and Heddle earned gold in the Double and took home silver for their part in the Quad event.

McBean's accumulation of medals may well have continued but a back injury forced her to withdraw from the 2000 Olympics in Sydney, Australia, and brought to a halt her participation in international competition. Yet, when McBean talks about her rowing career, she talks not about what she did for rowing, or about the debilitating back injury, but what rowing did for her. One of the greatest life lessons she has learned, she maintains, is the importance of communication — and she learned that from rowing.

Born in Vancouver in 1968 and raised in Toronto, McBean started rowing in 1985 and the next year began competing with the junior national team. During her high school years, she was a "jock of all sports," she says, participating in basketball, soccer and volleyball: "Rowing was just the next thing I tried. I liked rowing and wanted to keep doing it.

"It's like when you're dating someone," she adds. "Why do you stop with one person? Because that person is right."

McBean started out as a sweep rower. In sweep rowing, each crew has an equal number of port and starboard rowers, and each rower has one oar. McBean was sweep rower on the starboard side in the bow, making her responsible for verbalizing strategy and tactics in the boat.

A hard-driving athlete, McBean always made great demands on herself — and those around her. "I would take it upon myself to try and make everyone in the crew competitive and aggressive — like me," she recalls. "I did a lot of talking at my team mates."

In 1990, at the end of that year's World Championship season in Tasmania — McBean's second year on Canada's national rowing team — her coach took her aside. His message was harsh: her team mates didn't want to row with her.

McBean was devastated. "My dream in this sport," she says, "was to be the type of rower with whom people wanted to row." So, she had focussed on her strength and rowing technique, assuming that would make her a desirable team mate. Only after her coach spoke to her did she realize she had treated some crew members badly. "I just wasn't an enjoyable person to have in the crew," she admits.

"The toughest thing I ever had to deal with was being told by my coach that people didn't want to row with me," she recalls. "It left me feeling nauseous."

McBean's desire to succeed, however, forced her to do some soul-searching. She had to admit to herself that she had been talking *at* her team mates, not talking *to* them, and that her approach did not include respect for others. "I was trying to push them the way I was pushing myself," she says in hindsight. "I was being bossy and naggy.

"Outside of the boat, I think, we all were fine with each other," she adds. But inside the boat, in the "work" environment, McBean's behaviour had to change. In competitive rowing, she realized, strength and technique were not enough; if she was going to win in a team sport, she had to be able to communicate with her team mates and inspire them with her passion and drive. She had to become "a better person."

"The coach's comments definitely were what resonated with me the most," she says, "and what, without question, motivated me to change."

In 1991, a pre-Olympic year, McBean resolved to be more careful. She resumed training with Heddle, whom McBean considered the best portside rower in the world. To build winning momentum, McBean knew she not only had to be the best starboard rower possible but she also had to ensure that Heddle wanted to work with her. "When you don't like the people you work with, it affects the quality of your work," she says. "Just because you're good at what you do doesn't mean that people are going to want to be a on a team with you."

That meant learning to communicate with Heddle in a way that made Heddle comfortable; to take into account the differences between McBean's all-out, outgoing personality and Heddle's quiet, private, reserved style; and, to accept those differences. "Kathleen will always do things slightly her way," McBean says, "and I will always do things slightly my way."

So, McBean came to accept that Heddle would not communicate with her in the same fashion as she communicated. "I started respecting that. It allowed me to stop trying to make Kathleen me," she recalls. "When I started letting Kathleen Heddle be Kathleen Heddle and stopped trying to communicate to her like Marnie McBean, we became stronger. When I stopped trying to make Kathleen into me, that's when we became world champions and set records."

That lesson was life-changing for McBean. Not only did she start winning medals, she learned a lesson that would hold her in good stead in her life after sport. "Communication is so key," she emphasizes. Communicating with team mates — or colleagues — does not mean haranguing them to perform, but means finding a way in which everyone can agree on the best team effort. "The idea of communication is making sure we're going in the same direction with the same purpose. It's about getting it done *our* way."

The back injury that dealt a temporary blow to her self-sufficiency — "I couldn't touch my knees let alone touch my toes," she recalls — and a permanent end to competition didn't end her contribution to rowing and Canada's Olympic athletes. A 1997 graduate of the Honours Kinesiology program at the University of Western Ontario in London, Ontario, she has worked closely with Canadian Olympic teams as a specialist in Olympic athlete preparation and mentoring in the 2006, 2008, 2010 and 2012 Olympic Games. Her goal is to enhance athletes' performances and build their self-confidence so they can compete successfully in the Olympic environment.

She is also a motivational speaker and one message she brings to her audiences is the importance of communication. "It's about building relationships and it is about understanding how the people around you help you and make you better," McBean says. "It's not about trying to make them give what I have. It's about trying to make them give what they have."

—◁○▷—

Mario Lechowski has had his share of hard knocks — literally — in his eight years as a professional boxer and lightweight champion. But although he calls boxing "one of the toughest ways to make a living," he doesn't regret one minute of his time spent in the ring.

"It's the only sport in the world that gets you prepared for life mentally," he argues. "Everybody should take boxing."

So, when Lechowski retired from the ring in 2004 at the age of twenty-five, he did what he believes in. He began teaching the sport at Florida Jacks Inc., a fitness club in downtown Toronto. He also introduced Counterpunch Promotions Inc., which twice annually stages the *Brawl on Bay Street*, a promotional event for financial services professionals who want to test their newly acquired boxing skills in the ring.

It was the right choice for Lechowski. "I love my job training people," he says. "I just don't want to fight anymore."

Turning your back on past glories is always tough, but it is especially tough for athletes who depend on physical prowess to excel at their sports. There is little they can do to stop the march of time and sometimes their bodies call a halt to their careers before their hearts and heads are ready. When Lechowski's time came, he was determined to make the transition gracefully.

Lechowski was born in Poland in 1979, moved to Spain in 1988 and arrived in Canada in 1990. He was living in Edmonton when he turned professional in 1996, at the age of sixteen, becoming the youngest professional boxer in Canada. "I like this," he remembers thinking at the time. "This is good stuff. I get to fight and nobody arrests me."

He fought his first title fight at the age of twenty on October 23, 2000; he lost that fight in a split decision to World Lightweight Champion Tony Pep. But a year later, Lechowski fought Pep again. This time the outcome was different: Lechowski become Canadian Lightweight Champion, a triumph that he counts as his greatest success. He lost that title in 2002 to Billy Irwin. By the time Lechowski decided to leave the world of professional boxing in 2004, he had won fourteen bouts, lost six and suffered two technical knockouts. He was at the "enough is enough" stage.

"The most important reason for leaving," he says, "is when you get in the ring, you are afraid to lose."

Lechowski figures even the best-trained athlete may not have what it takes to become a boxer: "If you don't like the pain and you don't have the heart for it, there is no way you are going to make it."

However, when Lechowski left the ring, he had to grapple with the little matter of making a living. He had seen too many former boxers — and other athletes — get lost in dreams of past glories and not be able to move forward. He refused to get caught in that trap. Past glories don't pay the bills, he says. He chose the entrepreneurial route and embraced a proven principle. "You have to stick to what you know," he argues. What he knows is boxing.

So, he began teaching boxing. He may have started with just two clients but now he is solidly booked with clients or classes at Florida Jacks. And, although he does train several professional boxers, they are not his main focus. He numbers actors and professional hockey players amongst his clients, as well as a number of normally pin-striped financial services executives and lawyers, thanks to the promotional efforts of the *Brawl on Bay Street*.

"Everybody should take boxing," Lechowski enthuses. The nature of boxing makes an individual more alert, more self-aware and more self-confidence "You're stronger. You're ready for life. You're not afraid to walk down the street." He rounds out the argument by pointing to the mental benefits of boxing, suggesting that it makes you stronger mentally.

It has certainly worked for Lechowski. Because of his passion, he found a way to make his past the platform for his future.

LEARNED SO FAR

- The purpose of communication is to make sure everyone is going in the same direction with the same purpose.
- The people around you help you and make you better.
- Being mentally strong makes you ready for life.
- Stick to what you know when you are starting a business.

CHAPTER THREE

Breaking the shackles:
How Lucille and Edward
tackled crippling debt

Debt, n. An ingenious substitute for the chain and whip of the slave driver.

— AMBROSE BIERCE, *THE DEVIL'S DICTIONARY*

It seems as if Canadians are taking inspiration from the grasshopper of *Aesop's Fables* and enjoying the pleasures of summer, rather than following the ant's example and putting away food for winter.

By December 2009, household debt in Canada had reached a new high of $1.41 trillion. That means, notes a 2010 report from the Certified General Accountants Association of Canada, entitled *Where Is the Money Now: The State of Canadian Household Debt as Conditions for Economic Recovery Emerge*, each Canadian held $41,740 in outstanding debt in 2009, more than double the amount of individual debt in 1989. In fact, the report continues, the level of debt — adjusted for inflation and population growth — shows a continuous upward movement over the past two decades.

The worst of it is that consumer debt seems to be the culprit. To quote the report again: "The share represented by revolving credit (personal lines of credit and credit cards) within total consumer credit issued by chartered banks grew to 77.7% in 2009, from 21.1% in 1989. Borrowing through personal lines of credit increased twenty-five-fold within this period of time."

Like Lucille and Edward, in the pages that follow, Canadians are substituting consumption from income with consumption from credit — and paying the price. And just as mounting interest charges compound debt, financial problems compound personal problems. Bone-crushing debt affects relationships, stress levels and outlook on life. Just ask Lucille and Edward.

—<o>—

Long-time Canadian resident Lucille is a transplanted Pennsylvanian who makes her home in a rural area of Western Quebec. Her ancestors have been "kicking around" North America since the 1600s, she says, and fought in the American War of Independence in 1776, making her a proud member of the Daughters of the American Revolution. It also gives her an appreciation of the past.

Lucille is a serial abuser of credit. Her financial history includes several brushes with bankruptcy, all of them leaving her sense of humour more intact than her bank account. "I keep bailing my ass out of trouble," she admits, laughing ruefully at the memories. Jobs such as a security guard with a gallery and an art director for a film company brought in income while careful cost-cutting made ends meet. "I think the worst was when I ran away from home when my youngest child became a legal adult," she says, referring to her decision to leave home and husband when her son turned eighteen years of age.

But now, Lucille is seventy-two years old — an age when she would like financial security. Instead, she finds herself $50,000 in debt, owner of a dollar-sucking, 150-year-old stone house and an underperforming investment portfolio. She admits to anxiety and indecision about how to buy back her future: "I wake up thinking 'Oh my God, how do I get out of this one?' The little adding machine up there — it keeps coming up in a huge, red bottom line."

Lucille's latest debt issues rose out of her love of "flipping" houses, an avocation she has followed off and on since 1963. "I like flipping houses," she says, "going in and buying a house and fixing it, then buying another house." She calls it a "labour of love."

"I fall in love with houses," she adds with a smile. "I think, 'Here's this poor house that really needs something done to it,' which is always a dangerous thing to do."

She is licensed to sell real estate and her real-estate training and general savvy have enabled her to get houses at good prices. And she enjoyed a certain amount of success until her sense of history got the better of her and she fell in love with a 150-year-old stone house about an hour's drive from Ottawa. Since then, maintenance, heating expenses and cost of repairs have steadily risen — at the same time as her income from her investment portfolio declined by one-third, a victim of the volatile markets and stumbling economy of 2008-2009.

As well, Lucille admits to a certain amount of "indolence." She has resisted finding a part-time or even full-time job to help her cash flow. "I don't feel like going out and standing in Housewares," she admits, referring to the low-paying jobs that might be available to her.

Maybe it is a case of older and wiser, but Lucille's debt situation is causing her to do some soul-searching about the nature of debt and her — and others' — propensity to get into debt. Maybe it's one part optimism, she says: individuals often have a tendency to deny their debts, glossing over them, until the time of reckoning. She cites as her example Dr. Pangloss, a central character in Voltaire's *Candide*. In this 1759 satire, Dr. Pangloss maintains his unrealistic optimism about life in the face of huge evidence to the contrary. After all, "all is for the best in the best of all possible worlds."

Then there is that "certain sense of entitlement," that "I am worth it" attitude. Lucille equates entitlement with a kind of greed for material possessions that an individual does not genuinely need. "We tell ourselves, 'I am such a grand person. I've worked hard, so I can buy these toys; I deserve all of them!'" she says. "One does not have an entitlement to go and get something because one wants it and feels one deserves it — if you can't pay for it. I think that has been a huge part of this whole problem."

No one is entitled to be a spendthrift, she insists, a lesson she has learned through experience.

Now, Lucille is facing some tough decisions. In the near term, she can renegotiate her mortgage and downsize her mortgage payments, freeing up enough cash to allow her to pay down some debts. She can also lower the cost of heating her 150-year-old home by boosting energy efficiency. She can ask the heating company to amortize the cost of the expensive repairs through the equalized billing process, which would soften the immediate impact of the high repair bill. She has a list of other money-saving measures for her lifestyle, such as shopping for groceries on a needs-only basis.

That will keep her afloat for the time being. In the longer term, however, the decisions are a little more life-changing. She has to decide if her "flipping" days are over. "I'd like to do something that's a little less strenuous. I keep falling off ladders," she says, making a joke about a serious situation.

She could sell her treasured stone house and downsize. But that means moving yet again. She could get a home equity loan from the bank, but it would be another debt and when she sold the house — whenever that might be — she would have to repay the loan. It seems like more of a short-term solution than a long-term solution.

"I have to make adjustments," she acknowledges. She just hasn't determined which adjustments. But she is resolved to get her finances — and her life — in shape.

It may have been slow coming but she has learned a lot about handling debt — knowledge she is happy to share. She advocates control over spending, a rational approach to projecting costs and benefits for projects, such as her stone house, and the importance of budgeting both on-going expenses and one-shot project expenses.

"Examine well in advance of spending whether you can actually afford a large cash outlay," Lucille advises. "Be realistic about how much cash you should have on hand for emergencies and avoid biting off more than you can chew."

◄○►

Half a continent away, Edward and his fiancé Susan are well on their way to shaking off the shackles of debt. For this thirty-something couple, the catalyst was starting a family. "We've talked about it," Edward says, "and we don't want to have kids until we're financially in a position to have kids."

That meant coming to terms with the $36,000 in debt they had accumulated and making some tough life choices. First off, they had to leave the grasshopper lifestyle behind and behave more like ants. "You only live once," says Edward, "but you also have to think about those things that are happening in the future. Are you having kids? Do you want your kids to live a comfortable life?"

Edward's and Susan's about-face came in November 2009, but not before they had reached the crisis point. The mounting debt and the overdue interest charges were putting stress on their relationship. "I always got a little bit on edge whenever we talked about money," Edward concedes, "especially when we wanted to do things together or needed to buy anything. I hit a spot where this was getting out of control."

Both Edward and Susan had student loans, but Edward, particularly. He had spent two years at McMaster University in Hamilton, Ontario, before abandoning his studies in 2001 to travel. When he returned from his travels, he attended University of Western Ontario, in London, from 2003-2005. On top of student loans, Edward had run up $6,000 in credit card debt traveling. "I lean toward the belief that you only live once," he admits. "That's why I went traveling when I did. I never really thought about the repercussions until after I was deep into the hole."

Then, add on the bar and restaurant bills of a young couple attending university, it all added up — to $36,000.

So, Edward and Susan set about putting their financial house in order. Their first decision was moving to Western Canada in September 2009. Short term, the move added to their expenses, but longer term, it reduced expenses. "By making this move," Edward says, "we found ourselves not doing nearly half of the bar and restaurant stuff. So, we ended up saving a ton of money."

Edward found a job working for a financial institution in October 2009 and, a month later, Susan found a social work job. That took care of the income side of their financial statement.

They then turned to getting their everyday spending under control. Although Edward bemoans the lack of financial education in school, he did know enough to track expenses and make a budget. The couple entered all their expenses — fixed expenses such as rent, utilities and food as well as variable expenses such as entertainment — into a spreadsheet. They tracked *all* expenses. "We track absolutely everything; nothing goes unaccounted for," Edward insists. "If we go to 7-11 and get a Slurpee we'll budget that." The net effect: they became very aware — and subsequently, very careful — about what they spent.

Edward has also become very adept at cost/benefit analysis. He now calculates the cost of buying something on credit on the basis of how many hours he will have to work to pay off the interest. Air travel is a good example: when weighing the cost of traveling by air, he factors in how long he has to work to pay the higher cost of air travel, plus the amount of interest that will accrue on his credit card balance.

"That's a few hours work," he explains. "I never really processed that."

Edward and Susan also developed a three-year plan. Now, they both put their salaries into a joint account; they each withdraw $50 a week for personal expenses. The remainder pays shared expenses such as rent and groceries as well as $700 a month that goes to pay down debt. The emotional payoff for the couple: watching the decreasing debt level.

Edward and Susan are well on their way to reaching their goal: being in a financial position to have a family. And the couple have learned a lesson that will stick with them: today's spending decisions affect their future dreams and well-being. Edward and Susan are determined to live within their means, so they can afford the things they really want.

LEARNED SO FAR

- No one is entitled to be a spendthrift.
- Today's spending decisions affect future dreams and well-being.
- Track your expenses; do a budget. Live within your means.

CHAPTER FOUR

Escaping the bonds of addiction: How Arthur Sutcliffe and Erin Curtis got clean

A horrid alcoholic explosion scatters all my good intentions like bits of limbs and clothes over the doorsteps and into the saloon bars of the tawdriest pubs.

— DYLAN THOMAS

Arthur Sutcliffe and Erin Curtis (not their real names) struggled for years to free themselves of the devastating effects of alcoholism. They risked their families, their health and their futures. They each became someone they couldn't have imagined before alcohol took control of their lives. Both were on a downward spiral, until they sought help and understanding from Alcoholics Anonymous.

—<o>—

Over the course of twenty-five years, Arthur Sutcliffe dug himself deeper into alcoholism and drug addiction, along the way endangering his marriage, his young child, his career and his health. He was "hopeless" and "dying," he admits, until 2003, when at the age of forty-six, he took the steps he needed to turn his life around. He stepped into Alcoholics Anonymous (AA).

Clean since then, Sutcliffe has become a strong advocate of AA's "12 Step" program. "The whole point behind the 12 Steps is to facilitate a spiritual experience among the hopeless," he explains. He has found hope and peace and he holds on to that by bringing the 12 Steps to other alcoholics and drug addicts who have lost hope.

"When I started caring more about the other person's sobriety and well-being than my own," he says, "mine was always taken are of."

Sutcliffe's path to alcohol abuse is one often travelled by young people. A self-described "introverted, geeky, awkward young man," Sutcliff felt out of place when, in 1977 at the age of twenty, he moved to Lindsay, Ontario, to attend community college. As he studied toward a Fisheries and Wildlife Technician diploma, he joined some classmates for a pub night, sampling his first rum and cola. It tasted so good — and he enjoyed himself so much — that he had more than a dozen drinks that evening.

Sutcliffe was seduced by the way alcohol made him feel and he graduated to experimenting with drugs. By 1982 he was heavily using LSD and PCP as well as alcohol; he hit his first bottom at the age of twenty-five. Sick with pneumonia, broke and evicted, he returned to his parents' home in Burlington, Ontario. "I was literally dying," he recalls.

But it was a short respite. A week later, he was back drinking and taking drugs. By 1985, he was working in marketing in Toronto's financial district by day, and drinking, injecting cocaine, smoking marijuana and occasionally indulging in LSD by night.

Two years later, Sutcliffe hit bottom for the second time. That established the pattern that would mark the next eighteen years of Sutcliffe's life. "During the day, I'm in a three-piece, pin-stripe suit," he says. "At night, I'm in commando fatigues running around with prostitutes and murderers and drug dealers, shooting needles into my arms."

He'd hit new lows and limit his use, but any respite was temporary. He married, had a child, held a job, but the essential pattern didn't change. All he cared about, he remembers, was: "How do I get high? How do I stay high? How do I get higher?"

In one episode, he woke in a drug-induced stupor to find his three-year-old son and a playmate playing squirt-gun with his dirty needles. "I felt like **** as a dad," he admits. "But it never caused me to stop.

"I'm sitting in a basement apartment with a guy I don't even know, sharing a dirty needle with him, thinking I'm dying here. And I knew I was going to use again."

It was a downward spiral. By the late 1990s, seemingly unimportant events would trigger what Sutcliffe describes as "blind, murderous rages." "I would suffer from black, deep, dark, manic-depressive moods that would last weeks or months," he says. "I'd be left in a hateful, murderous spirit."

In 2001, he was diagnosed with early liver disease. By that time, the drinking, drugs and other indiscretions had put his marriage at risk, ruined his health and cost his independent marketing company untold business. Sutcliffe knew he couldn't live with drugs but was having a hard time living without them; he knew he was emotionally, spiritually and financially bankrupt. That was when he turned to AA.

Sutcliffe remembers meeting an AA member in a coffee shop; the member coached him through the 12 Steps to what Sutcliffe believes was a spiritual experience, which he defines as becoming "God-conscious." That, he says, triggered a "personality change sufficient to bring about a full recovery from alcoholism and drug addiction."

The 12 Step program requires an individual to admit that he or she has become powerless over alcohol and drugs, that life has become unmanageable. Recovering alcoholics must also admit to their wrongdoings and resolve to make amends. Most important, perhaps, the program places a strong emphasis on spiritual experience, including acknowledgement of the place of a Higher Power in the alcoholic's recovery.

The spiritual experience, Sutcliffe says, removes the urge to drink or take drugs: "I've duplicated that experience with alcoholics, drug addicts, gamblers, sex addicts, food addicts, co-dependents and self-harm addicts. Their human resources — their own strengths, family, friends, doctors, psychiatrists and others — have utterly failed them. They're dying and they know it. Nothing works — treatment, counselling, therapy, divorce, abstinence — they always find a way to go back."

So, Sutcliffe facilitates the spiritual experiences of other alcoholics and addicts, thereby reinforcing his own determination to avoid these substances. Caring about the sobriety of the individuals whom he counsels enables him to deal with his own drug and alcohol issues, he believes.

"When I started caring more about the bottom-of-the-barrel, hopeless, disgusting crack addicts who would rob me blind at the first chance they get, and helping them get well," he says, "my sobriety was always taken care of." He fears he would return to substance abuse if he lost the opportunity to work with recovering addicts.

The combination of spiritual help, AA and helping others has worked for Sutcliffe. He has not touched alcohol or drugs in seven years. He has his life back — his marriage is on firm footing and he has rebuilt his marketing business — and his health is stronger. He no longer suffers from the black rages that marked his drinking and drug-taking periods and his liver has partially recovered.

"I have led such a joyous, happy life these past seven years," Sutcliffe says. "I wouldn't trade it for anything."

◄o►

Erin Curtis's battle with alcoholism took a different shape than Arthur Sutcliffe's. Driven by low self-esteem, she would find herself in an unhealthy romantic entanglement. When the relationship busted up, she'd increase her alcohol consumption, further feeding her feelings of inadequacy. The more she drank, the more likely she was to lose her job, and the more it felt like her life was spinning out of control. The pattern would begin again, as she'd fall into another unsuitable relationship. Twice she got pregnant; twice she terminated the pregnancy, amplifying her feelings of self-loathing.

But like Sutcliffe, when she had fallen as low as she could go, she found the strength to turn her life around. At twenty-nine years old, in July 2008, Curtis turned to Alcoholics Anonymous.

"I think that the guilt, shame and remorse I felt after having that second abortion just put everything into high speed," she recalls two years later. "It brought me to my bottom quicker."

"What I had lost was my self-respect, my self-confidence, my love for myself," she explains sadly. "I didn't really have any of those things."

Montreal born and raised, Curtis has always been something of an adventurer. In 1999, when she was nineteen, she headed to Hong Kong to work. She returned home to attend Concordia University and graduated with a degree in Design for Theatre. But she had liked the Far East; so, after graduation, in 2003, she spent six months traveling throughout Asia, including Thailand, Laos, Cambodia and Vietnam. "We did a bit of a *Heart of Darkness* thing," she says, referring to Joseph Conrad's novel that became the basis for Francis Ford Coppola's landmark film, *Apocalypse Now*. "It was great."

She returned to Canada in August 2003 and resumed a relationship she had begun before leaving on her trip. But Curtis had concluded that the kind of marriage that her parents had enjoyed was out of her reach; that relationship broke up and she took her drinking up a few notches. So, the cycle began.

Three years later, Curtis had just started a public relations job in Toronto when she discovered she was pregnant. On her first day at the job, she felt ill; that evening, two home pregnancy tests confirmed it. Although she admits she was shocked and scared, she knew she didn't want to become a mother; she was in "a really ugly relationship," she says, and was afraid of her partner. She thought her only way out was having an abortion.

"I always thought I wasn't going to be that girl," she says sadly. She returned to Montreal to terminate the pregnancy.

She became pregnant for the second time in early 2008 while in relationships with two partners, one of them married. "I was really in an ugly state," she admits. "I was going down fast and I ended up getting pregnant again."

This time, however, Curtis resolved to stop drinking and keep the baby. "There was no way I was going to be that girl again," she says. She began to see this pregnancy as a second chance, an opportunity to clean up her life and lead a responsible life as a mother, to show her parents and the world that she could raise the baby. And, perhaps, she could achieve some redemption for the first abortion.

"My life had been such a mess," she says. "Because of my lifestyle choices I had been drowning for the past year and a half with my drinking." She believed she could break the cycle.

But another part of her wasn't buying it. Despite her guilt at having a second unwanted pregnancy, she knew she could not face the commitments of motherhood. She couldn't support herself and her child financially and emotionally and deal with her alcoholism. "I was really sad," she says, "because I knew in my heart of hearts that I couldn't go through with it."

Curtis had her second abortion in April 2008 at a Toronto women's clinic and a few weeks later resumed her heavy consumption of alcohol. "I had a hard time facing the fact that I was that girl who had had two abortions, who didn't learn anything the first time around," she explains. "I think I drank because I didn't want to feel anything."

She also re-established her relationship with one of the men whom she had been seeing when she became pregnant. "My self esteem was so low at that point," she says with disbelief, "that I invited him back into my life. We would get drunk and romanticize the idea of being parents together — that's how sick it was. It was just a really sick time in my life.

"I was just so hopeless," she adds. "This was the life that I had created for myself and I didn't want to live it."

She joined AA in July of that year and she has not had any alcohol since.

Curtis credits her membership in AA and her relationship with her sponsor — the AA program includes a sponsor who acts as mentor and sounding board, both for navigating AA and life in general — for her turnaround. She is learning to accept the consequences of her decisions, to forgive herself. AA meetings, she says, helped her look at her situation and deal with the anger that resulted from the two abortions and other disappointments in her life. It brought closure which allowed her to begin loving herself.

"It's easy for us to hate ourselves, to beat ourselves up," Curtis says. "You're not a bad person. At the end of the day, abortion is a life choice — but it doesn't define your life. Just have that separation and love yourself."

LEARNED SO FAR

- There is help for you; you just have to seek it.
- By helping others you can help yourself.
- You must love yourself before you can love others.
- Do not let the guilt of past decisions haunt your present.

CHAPTER FIVE

Reconciling the public and the personal:
How David Crombie, Carol D'Amelio and Taylor Train turn challenges into opportunities

"Inspiration is not the exclusive privilege of poets or artists generally. There is, has been, and will always be a certain group of people whom inspiration visits. It's made up of all those who've consciously chosen their calling and do their job with love and imagination... Their work becomes one continuous adventure as long as they manage to keep discovering new challenges in it."

— NOBEL PRIZE LECTURE OF POET WISLAWA SZYMBORSKA
WINNER OF NOBEL PRIZE IN 1996

In few careers is there as great a dichotomy between what you have to do to get the job, and what you do once you have it, as there is in politics. Anyway you look at it, tying your professional ambitions to the whims of the public is an uphill battle. No wonder many consider politics a blood sport, in which people don't necessarily wait until you turn your back to stab you.

Yet, honourable people become politicians because they want to make a difference. And they do. David Crombie has made his mark in both municipal and federal politics, while Carol D'Amelio has made her way in the local arena. Taylor Train is an aspiring Member of Parliament who has won the right to represent his party in the next federal election. They have all had to endure unrelenting scrutiny as they do their human best to accomplish their goals and retain their ideals. And it is their openness to change that allows them to do that: all three embrace challenge as an opportunity to learn.

◄○►

David Crombie certainly has had his share of learning opportunities in the twenty years he spent in the political arena. He entered municipal politics in 1970 at the age of thirty-four when, after a nine-year stint at Toronto's Ryerson University, first as a professor and then as director of student services, he became a City of Toronto alderman. Two years later, despite being inexperienced and up against strong contenders with seasoned campaign organizations, he ran for mayor.

"I was so green I called a press conference on a Friday afternoon," he recalls, with a laugh, "and no one showed up." But Crombie had things to say about the direction Toronto was taking and he was determined to say them; a run at the mayoralty provided the platform. Beyond all expectations, he won the campaign. He became Toronto's "Tiny Perfect Mayor."

Mediation was key to Crombie's time in the Mayor's office. "Mediation is not about compromise," he says. Rather it is about creating a new position that all parties can accept and for which they all feel ownership. "You find a place, and you do that by dialogue — and that's not a cliché," he adds. "You have to listen, because most people don't want to fight to the death; most people want to fight to some kind of solution."

In 1978, he became a Member of Parliament and served the next ten years in Ottawa, first as Minister of Health and Welfare, then as Minister of Indian and Northern Development and finally as Secretary of State. In 1983, he even took an unsuccessful run for leadership of the Progressive Conservative Party. Talk about a learning experience! After a year of hard campaigning, he arrived at the Party's convention with only 115 committed delegates but his perspective intact. "It was a really interesting experience," he says. "I met a lot of people, learned a lot about the country — and was happy."

Happiness plays a big role in Crombie's belief system, and it is clear that learning makes him happy — which may be one reason he can see challenges as opportunities. "You can't — for long — do something that either you don't like doing or you're not cut out for," he argues. "You're not going to make other people happy about what you're doing unless you're happy doing it."

His appointment as Minister of Indian and Northern Development is a case in point. Some political pundits interpreted the posting by Prime Minister Brian Mulroney as punishment for Crombie not supporting Mulroney's run for leader. Crombie didn't see it that way. He saw the appointment as a challenge, an once-in-a-lifetime experience. "I was learning and travelling and having a good time," he says, recalling trips to Moscow, Vladivostok, the Bering Strait and the Arctic. "It was a wonderful experience which you cannot get otherwise."

But by 1988, Crombie and his family had had enough of Ottawa. They returned to Toronto and Crombie immersed himself in the issues that meant so much to him as mayor. He was involved in the establishment of the Toronto Waterfront Regeneration Trust in June 1988 and, from 1994 to 1999, he was chancellor of Ryerson. In 2001, be became president and CEO of the Canadian Urban Institute and held that position until 2007. In 2003, he became chairman of the advisory council of the Nuclear Waste Management Organization and of the Toronto Lands Corp. in 2008. Recently, he was chief federal negotiator in the financial settlement with the Mississaugas of the New Credit First Nation over the 1787 Toronto Purchase claim.

Each new challenge has built on the accomplishments of the past and he has embraced each opportunity. "I have enjoyed all the work I have done," Crombie emphasizes. "And I'll do this until I die."

—<o>—

Carol D'Amelio first got involved in municipal affairs in the 1990s, when she lobbied — successfully — for a much-needed community centre in northeast Burlington, Ontario, where she had been a resident since 1988. She found satisfaction in helping people and improving the city. So, come 1995, she ran in a by-election. She has been a committed city councillor every since.

Like Crombie, she embraces the opportunity to learn. "I'm a teacher," she says. "Teachers are learners. I expect to learn something everyday and be wiser for it."

And like Crombie, she doesn't shy away from a challenge. In early 2010, she decided to run for mayor of Burlington in the October 25 election, which she lost.

"Elections are the most difficult or challenging thing," says D'Amelio. "An election campaign is apart and different from the job of being a councillor. You have to sell yourself, and it's very important that people see the right qualities in a person."

Born and raised in Montreal, D'Amelio became a school teacher in 1966 at the ripe old age of nineteen. She subsequently did a degree in mathematics and psychology at Acadia University in Nova Scotia. "That's where I learned that things change and I have to learn to change with them," she says. "I have to be able to adopt and, sometimes, I have to initiate the change."

Certainly, she is no stranger to change. In 1981, she and her husband moved with two small children in tow — a third child was born there — to Saudi Arabia. They lived there until 1987. Learning a new culture and new customs added to her sense of tolerance and open-mindedness, she says: "We are what we absorb and learn. And we become better because of it."

When she is knocking on doors, she knows who she is, she has the loving support of her husband of thirty-seven years and she is not afraid to put herself out there. But she admits it is tough. "Going door to door is very difficult; you are putting yourself in the position of basically having a job interview at every door. Some people are not interested in hiring you at all, but you have to be able to appeal to all kinds of people. That is extremely challenging and requires a great deal of energy. It's very intense, and you have to be honest and put yourself out there.

"I love it," D'Amelio adds. "That's why I continue to do it. I'm inspired by people, and that's what makes things work for me."

◄○►

Taylor Train has yet to face his first election campaign as a candidate — but, in August 2010, he did win the nomination for Toronto's Parkdale High Park riding for the Conservative Party of Canada in the next federal election, whenever that may be. Whenever it is, Train knows he will be walking into the "lion's den."

"You have to be mentally and physically prepared," he says. "You have to have a belief in why you are doing this particular thing. You have to make sure that you are going into this not for yourself but for the people that you are going to represent."

A long-time party worker and campaigner, Train knows what he is talking about, even though this is his first foray as a candidate. Toronto born and raised, a graduate of Queen's University in Kingston, Ontario, in 1978, he spent a good part of his thirty-two-year financial services career working for insurance companies in the marketing and product-development areas. More recently, he spent four years working for financial services industry association Advocis, the Financial Advisors Association of Canada, with a focus on developing rigorous standards for Canadian financial advisors. In 2004 he joined the faculty of the Canadian Initiative for Elder Planning Studies, which specializes in the cultural aspects of aging, social gerontology, marketing and communication. He is also a director and lecturer at the Centre for Financial Services Excellence at Seneca College in Toronto.

But now, he says, he is at a different stage in his life. And he is pragmatic about the challenges ahead. He accepts that some battles cannot be won and that an honourable retreat is the only solution. And, when you're knocking on doors or reading media coverage, you can't take rejection personally.

"If you have thin skin, don't go to the party," he warns, acknowledging that for every ten doors that open to him, there'll be one voter who will dislike him for reasons that may never become clear, such as the voter who responded with "You're all thieves!"

"Some people are like concrete," Train concedes. "They're all mixed up and hard as rock."

To ensure that he can react gracefully in any situation, he has prepared his responses to a list of possible scenarios. "I'm going to become a machine. I'm going to program myself," he says. "In these circumstances, this is the way I will behave because you have absolutely no second chances to make a good first impression."

He is confident that his genuine concern will shine through, and he won't appear robotic. "I'm going to be the same Taylor Train," he says, "but I do have a very strong belief in compartmentalization."

Self-awareness also ranks high on the Train list of strategies for dealing with tough situations. It is a learning process that comes from carefully observing the world around you and learning from others' experience. It is also something that takes time and effort to achieve, he admits: "Self-awareness is a long-term thing. You have to be comfortable in your skin; your esteem has to be there."

Train has picked up the gauntlet, as have Crombie and D'Amelio before him, and is ready to turn challenges into opportunity.

LEARNED SO FAR

- Mediation is not about compromise; rather, it is about creating a new position that all parties can accept and for which they all feel ownership.
- You're not going to make other people happy about what you're doing unless you're happy doing it.
- Things change and you have to learn to change with them.
- Self-awareness is a long-term strategy.
- Chances of success increase when you are prepared.

CHAPTER SIX

Exercising their wills: How Dave Irwin and Gary Reinblatt rebuilt their lives

"God gave me a big gift. He gave me life. I don't want to give it up.

— DAVE IRWIN

On the surface, Dave Irwin and Gary Reinblatt have led very different lives. Irwin, a "Crazy Canuck," spent his career internationally, careening down mountains as a competitive ski racer; Montreal-born Reinblatt spent the better part of his career as a marketing executive for McDonald's Restaurants of Canada Ltd. in Toronto. But, dig deeper, and they share something very profound. Both suffered a major injury while skiing that changed their lives — and neither wasted a minute of recovery time feeling sorry for himself.

◄○►

Who can forget the Crazy Canucks? Known for their all-out speed and their take-no-prisoners style, Dave Irwin, Ken Read, Dave Murray and Steve Podborski did Canada proud in the 1970s. They never let the fear of crashing inhibit their drive for gold. Irwin competed in two Olympics and won the World Cup Downhill in 1975 and in 1980 was the winner of the North American Downhill Championship.

But crash they did. Irwin suffered his first head injury in the 1976 Olympics. "That first one was pretty bad," he admits. "But the second one — just before the 1980 Olympics at Lake Placid, New York — was four to six times worse. The third one, up at Sunshine [Village in Alberta's Banff National Park in 2001], well, it just compounded and compounded. Each injury has residual effects."

Irwin left the national ski team in 1982 but continued to compete in a few pro-am events and fundraisers each year, such as the Gerald Ford American Ski Classic Legends Downhill race, which he won in early 2001. A resident of Canmore, Alberta, where he has a souvenir and promotional products business, he was training for the Extreme Skier Cross at Sunshine on March 23, 2001, when he fell and hit his head. Even though Irwin was wearing a ski helmet, he suffered a diffuse axonal traumatic brain injury, the result of the brain moving back and forth in the skull, killing brain cells and causing swelling. He was in a coma for three days on life-support; the doctors didn't expect him to survive. He was only forty-six at the time.

On the fourth day, however, friend and former team mate Read was bedside. "Dave, open your eyes!" he demanded. According to Irwin's spouse, Lynne Harrison, Irwin opened his eyes. What Harrison remembers was the face Irwin made; a painter herself, Harrison recalls the painting by Edvard Munch called "The Scream."

"That was the face he made," says Harrison. "It was as if his mind had just come back into his body and he realized how much work he had to do. After a coma, you are in a reduced state of consciousness. But even then, Dave was aware of what was going on."

Irwin did have a lot of work to do. The right, top brain was severely injured and his physical movements were limited. As well, he had lost his short-term memory. He didn't recognize Harrison, who had been by his bed since the accident.

"He didn't recognize anybody," she says. "I didn't take it personally. It was part of the process."

"When you are brain-injured," says Irwin, "you don't know how much you don't know; you have to learn." He likens it to an eighteen-month-old child who doesn't know anything. "But that child has eighteen to twenty years to learn it. I had to relearn all of it. But I could pick and choose what I learned."

The early months of Irwin's recovery were taken up with the physical rehabilitation, going to physiotherapy, learning to walk, to coordinate his movements. "I just did it, inch by inch," he says. "You lift your right foot up, you put that foot down. You take your other foot, pick it up and place it ahead of the right foot." It never occurred to him he would do otherwise. It was his mandate to himself.

"I always have a mandate for myself," says Irwin. He started it when he was about twelve years old and growing up in Lomond, Ontario, near Thunder Bay. His dad was a builder, "big into house construction," like his grandfather before, and now his son. It was how he set his goals — and how he attained them.

Although he has made a strong physical recovery, he still doesn't do as much as he would like to do. He rides his bike and skis in the winter, but no longer runs. "I would like to do more," he says. "I am not quite ready and able in my head to get there, but I know I will get there."

The struggle to recover his short-term memory is more strenuous. He has progressed far more than expected, but he still has some distance to go. It is a work in progress. "About a month or so ago, I was doing exercises," Irwin says, "and getting phenomenal results."

If there is one thing that frustrates Irwin and Harrison, it is the attitude of the medical establishment. Irwin's recovery has far surpassed anything that was expected of him ten years ago. And the fact that he continues to improve defies conventional wisdom that improvement stops two years after an injury. Irwin acknowledges there have been improvements in treatment in the past twenty years, even five years: "But there is a long way to go before we understand the brain."

To address the issues surrounding acquired brain injury (ABI) in Canada, Irwin and Harrison established the Dave Irwin Foundation for Brain Injury in 2002. The Foundation raises money through donations and the annual Dash For Cash Ski and Snowboard Challenge. In 2010, Dash For Cash raised $40,000 (the 2011 Dash For Cash is scheduled for February

12 at Sunshine). Since its creation, the Foundation has raised more than $250,000.

That money then funds academic research into prevention, rehabilitation and treatment of ABI as well innovative outreach programs and services for people suffering from ABI. The Foundation also wants to raise public awareness. Irwin notes that the number of people affected by ABI continues to escalate. In Canada, statistics are assembled province by province. Ontario, Canada's most populous province, recorded 18,518 brain injuries in 2001: 12,046 were considered mild, 1,317 were moderate and 1,610 were noted to be severely brain injured. A total of 4,517 died as a result of a head injury.

"We want to remove the stigma of having a brain injury," says Harrison. "People don't know what to say or how to say it, so they disengage. When you go through tough stuff, you find out who your friends are."

For his part, Irwin is as unrelenting about his recovery as he was about his next ski race. He looks at how much he has recovered since 2001 and he is optimistic he will make a full recovery. "God gave me a big gift," he says. "He gave me life. I don't want to give it up. So, let's go do it. I am doing it — and that's important."

—◇—

Gary Reinblatt's date with fate was March 23, 1990. The then forty-four-year-old was skiing with his youngest son, twelve-year-old George, at Whistler Ski Resort in British Columbia. It was the last day of March break. Reinblatt remembers planting his ski pole — and waking up in the Shaughnessy Hospital in Vancouver completely paralyzed.

"Literally at that minute, I made a decision," says Reinblatt. "If I wanted to figure out how unlucky I was, I would never sleep another night in my life; or I could figure out how lucky I was, because if I had broken my neck a quarter of an inch higher, I would have died, then I wouldn't have slept another night in my life. So, I told myself, 'Go out there and see what you can do.'"

And that is what he did. He defied the odds and escaped the wheelchair and neck-brace; he walks with a walker, uses his arms to answer the phone. He plays bridge, travels the world, and attends sporting events and plays.

He sits on not-for-profit boards as well as for-profit boards. He has a new girlfriend. "I keep myself 100% active," he says.

Reinblatt grew up in Montreal in a family that knew the value of hard work. His father was nineteen when he immigrated to Canada from Europe. "My father never made a lot of money," Reinblatt says, "but he taught me one thing: never be afraid of life."

He graduated from what was then Sir George Williams University (now Concordia University) in 1967 and moved to Toronto to take a job. He did sales and sales promotion jobs and worked in an advertising agency until he landed the job that mattered. In 1969, he became McDonald's Canada's one-man marketing department.

By all accounts Reinblatt excelled at his job. By the time he stepped down in 1993, his department boasted twenty-five staff and McDonald's had grown to more than 700 restaurants from ten.

"Most important, I kept my life in balance," Reinblatt says. He was happily married to Sandra and had two sons. "I took vacations. I worked a lot of hours but not eighty hours a week. I was extremely productive; I worked smart. I had time to coach my kids' baseball and hockey teams. And not a single kid I coached learned anything about athletics from me. They learned about life.

"And it didn't hurt that I could take them all to McDonald's," he adds.

Reinblatt's accident shattered more than his spinal cord.

Injured between the third and fourth vertebrae, Reinblatt had control only of his head and neck. McDonald's flew him back to Toronto in a private jet and he spent the next year at Lyndhurst Hospital, a Toronto rehabilitation hospital. "My attitude was: I have a job; my new job is to get better. I worked my butt off."

To keep his brain going, he scheduled his visitors. He didn't want ten people one night and none the next. At first, he found, visitors came in pairs. "No one wanted to come and visit by him- or herself. They didn't know what to expect. I had about six minutes to prove I was the same asshole as I was before the injury," he jokes.

Reinblatt went back to work at McDonald's after his rehabilitation. But it was short-lived. "I knew what I could do and what I couldn't," he says.

"I didn't have the stamina. I needed help." But he still sings the praises of McDonald's and how well he was treated. "The people at McDonald's were unbelievable," he says.

Once he stepped down, the phone started to ring; people wanted his help. So, based on doing what he could do and what he wanted to do, Reinblatt started his next career. He is a motivational speaker and marketing consultant, who becomes "a different set of eyes" for selected clients.

But life is full of hard knocks and it had yet another one in store for Reinblatt. In 2004, Sandra, his wife of thirty-four years, was diagnosed first with colon cancer, then two-and-a-half years later, with a type of thyroid cancer. She died in 2007 at the age of sixty-three. It was a difficult blow for many reasons but not least because he relied on Sandra for the help he needed to maneuver through each day.

Bur Reinblatt only knows one way to move — and that is forward. He has a girlfriend, whom he met playing bridge. He has resumed his travels, now that he has a companion. He is certainly not wasting time feeling sorry for himself. "Everyone has their own problems," he says. "God helps those who help themselves."

Reinblatt made an amazing journey back to mobility because he "willed" it. And every day is both a challenge and a triumph. "Everything works," he jokes, "and nothing works right."

So, what does attitude have to do with the healing process? As Reinblatt was told by his physician: "Medically, not a thing. In reality, everything."

LEARNED SO FAR

- Never be afraid of life.
- When recovering from an injury, you have only one job — to get better.
- God helps those who help themselves.

CHAPTER SEVEN

Letting go of the past:
How Galit Solomon
moved forward

"I left pieces of myself in that living room on that day that I will never be able to reclaim. For the twenty years or so that followed, I just wanted to figure out a way of reclaiming those pieces. But at the age of thirty-two, I realized that I might not ever be able to reclaim those pieces."

— GALIT SOLOMON

Galit Solomon joined the CTV Television Network news team in Toronto in 2004 at the age of twenty-eight. She has tackled heart-breaking stories such as the Toronto area wife and mother who aspired to be an Olympic torch bearer despite having terminal cancer, and the abduction and eventual death of nine-year-old Cecilia Zhang. As an Israeli-born Jew of Indian heritage growing up in multicultural Toronto, she prides herself on her professional detachment, her tolerance and her commitment to tell the story objectively — and she has earned a string of awards that prove she can do just that.

But one story that challenges Solomon's sense of detachment is her own story. In 1988, when she was twelve years old, just before she and her family left Israel to come to Canada, she was sexually abused by the father of one of her friends.

The experience changed her, she admits. She felt she had to keep it secret and she felt isolated. She lost a lot of her ability to trust. "I was just frozen by what had happened," she says.

But in 2007, when Solomon was asked to host a gala for York Region Abuse Program, which deals with child sexual abuse and adults who were abused as children, she decided to share her wrenching experience and let her audience know she was a survivor.

In 1988, in anticipation of their move to Canada, the Solomon family had sold their home and moved in with Solomon's grandmother. Several weeks before the move, Solomon returned to her old neighbourhood in Lod, a suburb of Tel Aviv, to visit a close friend. Her friend was not at home, but the friend's father was and he suggested Solomon return in half an hour. When Solomon returned, he invited her into the house, a comfortable, and normal-enough occurrence, but he was wearing only a towel. The father, who was always affectionate with his children and with Solomon, asked for a kiss. She complied, with the traditional gesture of affection, a kiss first on one cheek and then on the other. She realized the danger too late.

"That's when the assault happened," she recalls. "It was brutal. I had no idea where it came from."

She remembers feeling like someone had picked her up and thrown her against a wall; yet, she didn't really understand what had happened. She also remembers thinking that she had to keep the incident a secret, for fear no one would believe her.

She did keep it a secret for four years, as her sense of guilt and anger built. But, at age sixteen, she confided in a high school guidance counsellor. The counsellor put her in touch with a social worker and several weeks later she began discussing it with her family.

"I didn't think it was possible for anyone to experience what I had just gone through," she says. "There was a certain amount of shame and guilt. I felt guilt. I felt like: why did I go in there?"

From all appearances, Solomon moved on. She attended York University and graduated with a bachelor's degree in English and Mass

Communications. Her broadcasting career began at a Toronto production company, and then continued at the television station the New VR as a reporter covering York Region. In 2004, she joined CTV Toronto's news team. While at CTV, she attended the Poynter Institute of Journalism in St. Petersburg, Florida.

But, Solomon says, she didn't really start "dealing with it" until she was thirty-two. That's when she sought professional therapy and began working with the York Region Abuse Program as volunteer. She took another step in the summer of 2010, when she filed a report with police in Canada for forwarding to Israeli authorities.

"I feel like I left pieces of myself in that living room on that day that I will never be able to reclaim," she says. "For the twenty years or so that followed, I just wanted to figure out a way of reclaiming those pieces. But at the age of thirty-two, I realized that I might not ever be able to reclaim those pieces."

Solomon continues to volunteer at Boost Child Abuse & Prevention and has received its Voice of Courage Award. She has also started a website to provide resources and contacts to sexually abused women. And when she counsels women in her situation who may not have begun dealing with the experience, she tells them that it is never too late to seek help. Freer and more open discussion will help everyone involved. For the male partners of abuse victims she counsels patience.

"Be patient. Be very patient," she explains. "It requires an awful lot of patience."

Solomon likes to think that patience will be rewarded.

LEARNED SO FAR

- There is no "picking up the pieces" of the past. There is only the future.
- Opening the trauma to the light begins the healing process.

CHAPTER EIGHT

The healing process:
How Lawrence Geller and Francis McNamara learned to live with disabling illness
How Brian McMillan steeled himself for his wife's battle with cancer

"You can't give up hope. If you do, your soul becomes bankrupt. You have to be able to go forward and know that tomorrow will be a better day than today."

— DR. HAROLD ROCKET, AUTHOR WITH RACHEL SKLAR OF *A STROKE OF LUCK*

Thanks to medical advances, contracting a serious disease is no longer a death sentence. More and more Canadians are surviving illnesses such as cancer or heart disease. But while chances for survival improve, the statistics indicate that many of us will probably experience a major disease. For example,

- An estimated 70,000 Canadians experience heart attacks each year; about 16,000 of them die as a result, with most of those deaths occurring out of hospital. That means, each year, 54,000 Canadians arrive in a hospital emergency ward and, thankfully, survive their heart attacks.

- An estimated 50,000 Canadians suffer strokes each year, with 36,000 Canadians surviving. The Heart and Stroke Foundation of Canada estimates some 300,000 Canadians live with the effects of stroke.

- In 2010, an estimated 83,900 Canadian women and 90,000 Canadian men will be diagnosed with cancer; 62% are expected to survive more than five years after their diagnosis.

- The Kidney Foundation of Canada estimates two million Canadians have kidney disease or are at risk. Each day, fourteen Canadians learn they have kidney disease.

If you're lucky — like Lawrence Geller, Francis McNamara and Donna McMillan — you'll live to tell the tale, but not before the fight to see another day tests the mettle of both you and your loved ones. As Geller and McNamara will tell you, the often traumatic lifesaving procedures you undergo are only one part of the experience; you have to learn to live with the residual effects of the illness. That requires you to bring to bear all the emotional and spiritual fortitude you have. And as Donna's husband, Brian McMillan, will testify, he may not have endured the physical consequences of treatment, but he, too, had to dig deep to provide the strength and solace his wife needed. They all developed strategies and new understandings that helped them through this test of time.

◄○►

Lawrence Geller believes that the way in which you deal with life and people determines the way you deal with trauma and its aftermath. His 2008 health crisis put his beliefs to the test.

Geller has always been a people person. As an insurance agent for six years, then president of his own agency, Campbellville, Ontario-based L. I. Geller Insurance Agency Ltd. for close to thirty years, his skill is finding practical solutions for people's financial problems. Practicing in Campbellville, a small town about seventy kilometres west of Toronto, he made his reputation by his actions. He is frank and honest, a respected member of both his local and professional community, a regular speaker at industry events and an advocate for his industry.

Yet, when Geller woke in the Acute Emergency Unit of St. Michael's Hospital in downtown Toronto at 4:00 a.m. on July 19, 2008, with intravenous tubes and leads to three machines sticking out of him, he was shattered. "That was the scariest part," he recalls. "I knew at that point what was happening. The toughest thing was lying in Emerg, with two nurses holding my hand, with the head of the ICU coming in and saying 'You're not going to die on my watch.'"

Previous to his visit to St. Mike's Emerg, Geller hadn't been feeling unwell. He admits feeling a little lethargic, and his doctor had warned him the previous December that his blood pressure was a little high. But a slight increase in blood pressure the following spring wasn't enough to cause Geller and his wife of twenty-eight years to cancel a planned holiday to France. But when Geller returned home — his wife continued on to Ireland — his housekeeper noticed that he was unsteady on the stairs and his assistant noticed his signature had become shaky. When Geller's wife returned home, they approached her with their concerns.

After initial tests and an appointment with a diagnostician, Geller ended up at St. Mike's. High blood pressure, as well as diabetes and cardiovascular disease, is a common cause of kidney disease. On July 23, doctors informed Geller that one kidney had completely ceased functioning and that the other one had sunk to 9% of normal operating capacity. The temporary solution was peritoneal or home dialysis.

Geller believes that living by the old-fashioned, golden rule — "Do unto others as you would have them do unto you" — softens even medical blows. And he put his beliefs into practice during his eight-day stay at St. Mike's. "Treating people well makes all circumstances better," he says. "From the very first nurse you meet to the last nurse you deal with, it is how you treat them that determines what sort of time you're going to have."

Throughout this and a later hospital sojourn, he made a practice of befriending doctors, nurses and fellow patients. He helped the nurses arrange flowers for the patients and prepared snacks for the younger patients. He especially made a point of telling jokes to lighten the atmosphere. He probably helped himself as much as he helped others.

"How you treat people really determines how difficult those times are," he says, "because other people can make your life much more difficult." The flip side of that coin: if you treat people well, they'll treat you well, and make a difficult time much easier. Geller tried never to forget to say "thank you," even for small kindnesses.

Being pragmatic is also a Geller trait. He recognized that, although medical personnel may by times inflict pain and discomfort, the vast majority of medical personnel whom he encountered were sincerely trying to help. "Taking it out on the people who are trying to help you," he admonishes, "is not going to get you as far as gritting your teeth and being nice to people."

While it may fall into the "easier said than done" category of coping, you need to focus on maintaining dignity, Geller advises, even practice a certain amount of stoicism. "What good does screaming do?" he asks.

In January 2009, forty-eight pounds later, doctors declared Geller a suitable candidate for a kidney transplant. His wife donated one of her kidneys and the operation took place on March 31, 2009. Geller likes to think living the golden rule got him through this difficult time — and, hopefully, his attitude helped others get through their own tough times.

◄○►

Forty-five-year-old Francis McNamara was on his home treadmill on December 23, 2009, when things started to go a little "wonky." Slight and fit, a runner, for the past month he had been going faster and faster on the treadmill, working toward doing a marathon. He slowed the treadmill, but he still kept listing to one side.

His concern was growing. He went for a drink of water, but the glass fell out of his right hand. He asked for a pen and discovered he couldn't write anything. "I knew something was seriously wrong," McNamara says. "I sat down on the bed and cried for a second."

But only for a second. He knew he had to do something and he wasn't going to waste time feeling sorry for himself. He and his partner David Harland set out for the emergency ward of Toronto's St. Michael's Hospital. It was there that McNamara "stroked out" and had a full hemorrhagic stroke.

A stroke occurs when blood flow to the brain is interrupted causing brain cells or "neurons" to die. There are two types of strokes: ischemic and hemorrhagic. Eighty per cent of strokes are ischemic strokes, when a blood clot interrupts the flow of blood; the other 20% are hemorrhagic stokes in which a blood vessel ruptures and there is bleeding into and around the brain. That is what happened to McNamara; it left his right side paralyzed and he was unable to speak, or at least not so anyone could understand him.

"I don't smoke, I don't do drugs, I exercise, I eat right," says McNamara, a real estate agent. "My cholesterol was fine, so was my blood pressure. I can't understand what happened."

The hospital didn't understand it, either, but it certainly knew what had happened. Harland was told to be prepared; the first twenty-four hours were crucial.

McNamara may have been partially paralyzed but there was nothing wrong with his hearing or understanding; one hemisphere of his brain was still functioning. He took all this in. "I decided that if I might die that night," he says, "I was going to stay awake all night long." He did: he listened in on the nurses' conversations; he also thought about his nephew, Craig, who, a month earlier, had fallen off a roof on Cape Breton Island, Nova Scotia, and died of head injuries.

"Craig was twenty-seven," McNamara remembers thinking. "I am forty-five. I have had a great life in Toronto this past twenty-four years. Craig will never have that opportunity." McNamara, a "Caper" himself, knew he could accept whatever came his way.

The next day dawned and McNamara perceived he was already getting better. "A lot of the time I didn't really think about it," he admits. "I took it for granted I would get better."

He spent a week in hospital, then six weeks in a rehabilitation centre, which may have been the hardest part for McNamara. It was a resident program, and although he lived a few blocks away, he had to spend week-nights in the centre. "I couldn't sleep in the hospital," McNamara says. "I shared a room with four older men. I couldn't find anybody my age with a stroke." So, he read instead of sleeping. "I read a book called *A Stroke of Luck* about a doctor, Dr. Howard Rocket, who had a full year of hell on earth. I realized I was well off. The book inspired me. I felt I was luckier than most."

He and Harland developed a routine. Usually, McNamara's therapy was in the morning; afterward, Harland would pick him up and bring him home, where McNamara could relax and sleep. Each evening, during the week, Harland would return McNamara to the hospital by 11:00 p.m. "David was a great supporter," McNamara says.

It may not have been the ideal situation but it worked. By late February, McNamara and Harland were in southern Africa for three weeks, touring South Africa, Botswana and Namibia with friends, a trip they had planned well before McNamara's stroke to celebrate their twentieth anniversary. McNamara hadn't recovered full sensory perception in his right leg, which meant he kept losing his right flip-flop without knowing it was missing. And there was still some pain in his right leg — but he was there. The excitement of being there chased other considerations from his mind. "We climbed the Cape of Good Hope," McNamara says. "I felt like Rocky when I got to the top."

McNamara still suffers residual effects of his stroke. His right side can be stiff; there is some pain in his right leg, but not enough to require medication. When he gets tired, talking can be difficult. But he takes "fifteen-minute supernaps" each afternoon. He is back selling real estate and recently painted the interior of their house. Sure, it took three months, but it was good exercise for his right arm. "I did it on my own terms," he says, which may be an apt description of how McNamara has adopted to life after a stroke.

"I figured by now I would be 100% better," he admits. "I may never get 100% better. It's an annoyance, but I can live with it. I am living with it."

—◁◦▷—

For Brian McMillan, his moment of truth came on April 28, 2010, as he and Donna, his wife of thirty-four years, sat in a Collingwood, Ontario, doctor's office, wrapping their minds around the implications of Donna's test results. Donna, who was fifty-three at the time, had been diagnosed with squamous cell carcinoma, a type of skin cancer, which, if left untreated, can spread among body organs. Typically, with squamous cell carcinoma, tumours appear on the exterior of the body as large, raw sores. In Donna's case, however, the tumours had moved into interior areas of the anus and rectum. Her prognosis was not good and she had weeks of aggressive treatment ahead of her at Princess Margaret Hospital in Toronto, more than 150 kilometres away from her family and friends in Collingwood.

Brian, then fifty-four, decided that the best way for him to cope was to be by his wife's side. He consciously focused his attention on his wife and shifted his attention away from his own concerns. "Basically, it's about her; it's not about me," he told himself. "It's not about how I feel about things — I'm not the person with cancer. I need to get beyond that."

That meant some organizational magic. First, they had to tell their four children, aged seventeen to thirty. An older daughter moved home from Calgary for the summer to help out. Then Brian, principal of McMillan Insurance and Financial Services in Collingwood, had to arrange backup at his financial planning practice, as well as leave from his position as president of the local branch of his professional association. The couple had to arrange temporary residence in Toronto; they decided that commuting between Collingwood and Toronto while Donna was in treatment wasn't a viable option. They could spend weekends at home in Collingwood.

Soon afterward, Donna began a gruelling series of treatments, five days a week for seven weeks at Princess Margaret Hospital. Given the spread of the cancer before detection, doctors downgraded surgery as an option. Instead, the plan called for a combination of chemotherapy and radiation therapy. But when it became apparent that Donna could not tolerate chemotherapy, the doctors elected to intensify the radiation therapy. Her treatment ended July 30, 2010.

For all his putting Donna's needs first, Brian didn't go through his wife's illness without support. The parts of Brian's life that sustain him day to day are God, his immediate family, what he terms his "church family" and his business as a financial advisor. And that didn't change during Donna's treatment. Brian turned to a close friend whose wife had survived the same type of cancer for insight. And he and Donna accepted the support of family, close friends and members of their congregation. He also relied heavily on staff at his Collingwood office to deal with clients and keep him informed about business matters while he was in Toronto.

Brian also found ways to reduce stress. During the treatment period, when he and Donna spent weekends in Collingwood, he made a point of having "projects" such as building a rock pond in the backyard. This became a form of respite, with their children taking over Donna's care. "Then, I was then able to go back," he explains, "and face it again for another week."

He also put Donna and himself into protective mode by sending regular email updates to concerned friends. That relieved the couple of constantly answering questions about Donna's condition. "You can write it in a journal form," Brian says, "so that people have a sense of what is going on without the telephone calls, without the visits and without having to relive it."

Donna and Brian are enjoying being back in Collingwood, their summer of commuting over. Early results showed some improvement. Once the effectiveness of the radiation treatment has been assessed, surgery may be a future option. In the meantime, the presence of the cancer in Donna's lymph nodes has been reduced and the McMillans are cautiously optimistic. Brian has come to believe that it was the daily mediation and prayers that helped him and Donna get past the denial stage and into the acceptance stage, which enabled them to deal with the crisis more effectively.

"If people don't have prayer, then they don't have faith," Brian says. "All they see is themselves, or their own ability, or the doctor's ability to make you well. It's really about acceptance."

LEARNED SO FAR

- Do unto others as you would have them do unto you.
- Treating people well makes all circumstances better.
- Count your blessings, whatever the circumstances.
- Find support in your circle of family and friends and in prayer.
- Understand the place of faith during a crisis.

CHAPTER NINE

Losing loved ones before their time:
How Denise Bellamy and Evelyn Jacks learned to live with loss

"A man's dying is more the survivors' affair than his own."
— THOMAS MANN, THE MAGIC MOUNTAIN

There is no escaping death; it is part of the human experience. Barring some significant scientific advance, we are all going to die, the only question is when. And there is a good chance some of us — or someone close to us — will die before our time. It is the way of the world.

But knowing that doesn't make it any easier for the person who is experiencing the agony of watching a loved one die before his or her time. The grieving person experiences many emotions — disbelief that this is happening, anger, guilt and, in time, acceptance. In time, the grieving person learns to live with the gaping emotional hole left by the death of a loved one.

Denise Bellamy and Evelyn Jacks have both lived through the pain of loss. Although it is never easy, Bellamy and Jacks survived. And they will both tell you there are steps you can take to lighten your load and progress toward acceptance.

"There is no right or wrong way to grieve," says Bellamy. "Everybody deals with it differently."

But, she adds, time does heal all wounds.

—◦—

Denise Bellamy first met Bill Thorpe in 1980. Bellamy was a thirty-one-year-old crown attorney for York Region in Newmarket, Ontario, north of Toronto, and Thorpe was a thirty-two-year-old police officer. The six-foot Thorpe was also a black-belt in judo and when the women in the Crown's office were threatened, he offered to teach a self-defense course. That was the beginning of a friendship that blossomed into a life-changing romance.

By the time Thorpe was diagnosed with terminal cancer on March 27, 1995, the two had a life together that included his two sons, a warm circle of friends, their golden retriever Chablis and a house in downtown Toronto. Thorpe taught aerobics at the YMCA, rode his bike thirty kilometres to work every day and honed his gourmet cooking skills. Bellamy was director of legal services at the Ministry of the Solicitor General and Correctional Services for the Ontario government and on an upward trajectory in her career.

"It was a complete shock," Bellamy remembers. "He was only forty-seven years old. He was so fit; he didn't smoke. I kept thinking, 'How is this possible?'"

But it was possible, and Thorpe's illness and death ten weeks later tested Bellamy in ways she couldn't have imagined. She survived the loss of her trusted friend and partner, in the process learning something about herself and the nature of grief, something she now shares with others.

Looking back, there were subtle signs that Thorpe's health wasn't all you'd expect in someone so fit. He had a cough, so his doctor put him on antibiotics for two weeks. He had headaches, but nothing debilitating, until one weekend the headaches were so bad he couldn't get out of bed. When he did sit up, he couldn't move his leg. Bellamy took him to the emergency ward at the local hospital. Within days, he was diagnosed with lung cancer that had metastasized to the brain; doctors told them he had six to twelve months to live.

"At the time, I felt very alone," Bellamy admits. "But, I told myself, 'I can't be the only person to have gone through this.' So, I started reading — books on cancer, books for caretakers of people with cancer, later books on grief."

A former colleague who had had breast cancer introduced Bellamy to Wellspring, a network of cancer support centres across Canada. There, she was introduced to a volunteer who did one-on-one counseling, well-known grief expert Dr. Mary Vachon. Bellamy began seeing Vachon once a week.

"Mary is the one who gave me the very best piece of advice — and which I now tell everyone," says Bellamy, "'Sometimes, one day at a time is too long to think about. Try ten minutes.' 'Yes,' I thought, 'I can manage ten minutes at a time.'"

Bellamy admits there were many times she was overwhelmed. Thorpe was in the hospital ten days and she was at his side from nine in the morning to nine at night. She was juggling Thorpe's care with her job and staff, friends coming to visit, family and friends who needed updating, and a dog that needed walking. When he came home, there were still regular visits to the hospital for radiation treatments, to shrink the four tumours in his brain to improve his quality of life. Home-care nurses visited twice a day and when Bill's son, Steve, finished university, he moved in to help.

"Every day, there was something else Bill couldn't do," Bellamy says. But he could still talk and the two talked about their life together, their love and his approaching death.

Thorpe died June 4. Tragically, his only brother had died the day before, from a ten-year battle with myeloma cancer.

"When Bill was dying," says Bellamy, "I was so busy, I had very little time to myself. After the funeral, once everybody had left and I was by myself, that's when the reality of my whole new life sunk in."

There were the practical things. Bellamy didn't know how to change the halogen light bulbs. "The house kept getting darker and darker," she jokes. And the question of food. Thorpe had done all the cooking, and although Bellamy became fixated on keeping the kitchen spotless, it didn't improve her cooking skills any.

Then there was the grief. "I was trying to see it as a normal part of the human experience," she says. But she was angry. An area not far from her home was a favourite hangout for local drunks. "How is it fair that they are still alive and Bill is dead?" she remembers asking herself.

"But, I refused to allow myself to stay angry," Bellamy says. "It's just not productive and, anyway, life isn't fair."

Bellamy was still seeing Vachon and through her, she joined a weekly group grief session organized through the funeral home. "I learned so much from that," she says. "There were people who were hurting more than I was. I learned from them and, at the same time, it provided me the opportunity to help other people."

It also gave her a way to measure her progress, as did keeping a journal. "What was happening to me was the most important thing that had ever happened to me in my whole life," Bellamy says. "It was all I wanted to talk about."

When she felt she was at risk of boring her friends, she wrote in the journal. When she needed someone to talk to at four in the morning, but was reluctant to wake a friend, she wrote in her journal. "Later, I found it comforting to go back and see how much progress I had made," she says. "Time really does heal all wounds."

Bellamy also kept a binder of pictures of Thorpe when he had been well — when they were traveling, or out cycling. When he died, she explains, he was skeletal: "I kept looking at the pictures in the binder until I no longer saw him as he had become when he was dying, but as a vibrant man."

Bellamy built her new life. In 1997, she became a judge in the Ontario Superior Court of Justice. Three years after Thorpe died, their financial advisor, Joan, died very suddenly. Bellamy shared what she had learned about living after losing a loved one with Joan's husband, Ian, lending him books and providing perspective. They fell in love and married in December 1999.

The couple retired in the summer of 2010 to travel and spend more time with each other and their grandchildren. They have both learned how precious each day together is. As Bellamy says: "We have been given the gift of time that our spouses were not. We have always tried to live that time with excitement and gratitude."

◄○►

It may seem to the casual observer that Winnipeg businesswoman Evelyn Jacks has everything going for her. Dynamic, focused, knowledgeable, she is the founder and president of The Knowledge Bureau, a national educational institute (and the publisher of this book). She, herself, is the author of more than forty books on personal taxation and wealth management; to millions, she *is* "Jacks on Tax."

Her expertise has been sought in many situations. In 2009, she was asked to be a member of the Task Force on Financial Literacy; previously the premier of Manitoba tapped her as a member of the province's Lower Tax Commission. On January 28, 2010, Jacks rang the bell that opened the Toronto Stock Exchange, to celebrate the launch of the "Tax Facts & Planning" section on its website *www.TMXmoney.com*. The Knowledge Bureau provides the content for the section, viewed by millions of investors each month.

It looks like Jacks is on a roll. But for the past decade, Jacks has suffered tremendous stress and loss in her personal life. In that time frame, she lost her father, her mother, her younger sister, her sister-in-law, her father-in-law and a trusted and honoured colleague to cancer, leaving her reeling emotionally. But, like Bellamy, she is finding her way through by digging deep into her personal strength and into the "circle" of support around her.

Jacks's beloved father was diagnosed with cancer at the age of sixty-six. Three years after her dad's death in 1998, her sister Elisabeth, affectionately known as "Betty," was diagnosed with late-stage breast cancer. Betty was only forty-three at the time.

"There are three girls in our family," says Jacks, "each three years apart. Betty is the middle sister." Jacks is the eldest of what was a very bonded sisterhood.

Jacks admits that both she and her mother experienced serious guilt, as if they, the older ones, should be the ones facing cancer and death, not the younger Betty. But it took only a moment before Jacks got her feet firmly on the ground. "Hey, wait a minute!" she recalls thinking. "This is not about you or me. Betty has this." She resolved that they would go through this together and that cancer would not get the upper hand. "Let's not let cancer take away our day," became Jacks's mantra. "We'll give cancer one hour a day, but the other twenty-three hours belong to us."

"It was a great coping strategy," she says.

The shiny, new convertible bought at the end of June also helped. As did the trips in between treatments — Cabo san Lucas, Mexico, for deep sea fishing, Ontario's Niagara wine region for wine-tasting, Singapore for a global business planning competition in which Jacks's son Cordell was competing, Europe to visit youngest sister Kathy and her family. Back home in Winnipeg, when Jacks's younger son Don played music gigs or lacrosse, the two sisters were generally there to cheer him on.

"If we were going to do this," says Jacks, "we resolved to do it in style! We made fabulous memories. Yet, we might not have done all those things if Betty hadn't had cancer — and the courage to embrace it the way she did."

That is not to suggest the family did not face up to facts. They had what Jacks calls "reality checks," when they sat down and faced their worst fears. Death wasn't the elephant in the room; they discussed its eventually, legal arrangements such as power of attorney, funeral arrangements, how they would communicate when Betty was in her final stages.

"We did life the rest of the time," says Jacks.

Jacks's determination to focus on life was severely tested, however. Out of the blue, her sister-in-law Bev, her husband's younger sister, was diagnosed with lung cancer. "There was one month when both Betty and Bev were having brain radiation at the same time," says Jacks. "We were scared, and with good reason." Bev died on October 29, 2008.

Betty was determined to make her fiftieth birthday. She did, triumphantly; Betty died at the age of fifty-one August 17, 2009. But three weeks before her death, after being at her daughter's side continuously, Jacks's mom, too, was diagnosed with cancer. The two women had been Betty's caregivers. Jacks would take Betty to doctors' appointments and cancer treatments; their mom would stay with Betty evenings, when Jacks would catch up with work.

"It was heartbreaking," Jacks says, with a catch in her voice, "that our mother had to endure watching her daughter die."

That wasn't the last of the bad news. On Boxing Day, her husband's father fell; shortly after Grampa Jacks was diagnosed with brain cancer. Once again, Jacks and her family were confronting the need to sustain two stricken family members — and each other. "My mother and father-in-law were in the hospice together," says Jacks. "Grampa Jacks died peacefully two weeks before my mom." Her mother passed away February 25, 2010.

Jacks admits that during this time she took solace from her business life, which, ironically, was booming. "My career life provided me with a reliable framework," she says, "around which to think over this long period of heartbreak and grieving."

There was one last shock in store for Jacks. She took most of March off to deal with estates and other personal and legal issues. When she returned, she felt stronger, ready to go ahead. Twelve days later, her colleague of twelve years, the woman who kept the Knowledge Bureau running like a well-oiled machine, Marion Trapp, died of cancer, too.

"It has been a time of great personal turmoil," says Jacks. "I haven't really had time to mourn these dear people. I feel like there has been a war with lots of casualties, and I have had to pick up the pieces and go forward."

But Jacks is a trooper. Even as she has experienced the darkness, she has kept her sights on the light. "Cherish the moment," she advises. "Make it fun. Tell stories and listen well. Laugh: it is the laughter that turns into the fondest memories."

Like Bellamy, she found not looking too far ahead helped her cope. "There is no need to think too far ahead," she adds. "We found that when things were overwhelming, we would just try to get through the next hour."

And like Bellamy, Jacks found she didn't need to go it alone. In her case, she turned to her "circle" of family and friends. The next generation — her sons and nieces and nephews — turned the tables and supported the older generation with their loving presence. "As you walk with the dying, it is important you draw on your circle and let them walk with you," Jacks says. "Our family was there for us."

That process triggered in Jacks a deep sense of gratitude and spiritualism, in its broadest sense, as she felt reassured that she was not alone. "Special 'angels' do come," she explains, "whether it is a loving hug, an unexpected note, a more intimate friendship or a telephone call. Whoever your higher spirit is, you become aware it is there, helping you.

"Grieving is a process," Jacks concludes. "You can't go over or around it; you have to get through it. Walking with people who are losing their lives is very painful. You are shell-shocked; everything around you is crumbling to rubble. But you have to find the energy to pick up the bricks. When you do, you will see that under them are new blades of grass. That is what you focus on, to carry on."

LEARNED SO FAR

- One day at a time is too long to think about. Try ten minutes.
- Live and build beautiful memories.
- Find help: read books, join groups or tap your circle of friends. There is no need to go through this alone.
- Grieving is a process and everybody grieves differently.

CHAPTER TEN

Making a difference: How Ken Singh and Dr. Aslam Daud brought aid to Haiti

"What I saw was extremely disturbing — that so many people were just out in the streets without homes, without food."

— DR. ASLAM DAUD

On January 12, 2010, an earthquake of 7.0-magnitude struck southern Haiti, with the epicentre just twenty-five kilometres west of the Caribbean country's capital, Port-au-Prince. In a matter of minutes, Haiti, already the poorest nation in the western hemisphere, was the scene of death and devastation. Buildings were leveled, power lines ruptured and thousands of people were dead or injured. As the dust settled, an estimated 230,000 people were dead, another 300,000 injured and one million were left homeless.

Television and newspapers captured the heart-wrenching images and people across the world shared in the tragedy. The outpouring of donations was outstanding — in fact, the Canadian government matched dollar for dollar its citizens' donations. Canadians were also there on the ground, putting aside their own emotional and physical discomfort and offering solace and hope to the injured and homeless. Ken Singh, president of Mississauga, Ontario-based Atlas Cargo Inc., and Dr. Aslam Daud, chairman of volunteer aid organization Humanity First Canada, were among the people offering aid.

◄○►

Ken Singh's commitment to Haiti is longstanding. A native of Guyana, a South American country that faces onto the Atlantic and the Caribbean basin, he connects Haiti to his heritage and his homeland. Over the years he has travelled to Haiti some twenty times, sometimes for business, sometimes bringing relief shipments of goods.

Running a shipping company gives him the means to do that. And, he admits, transportation is the only business he knows. Singh immigrated to Canada from Guyana in 1974 when he was in his mid-twenties and launched Atlas Cargo in 1986. Like so many entrepreneurs, he based his business venture on what he knew. "I pursued this career because that is the thing I started as a young man," he explains, including training with British Airways in Guyana. "That is the same thing I studied here in Canada."

But Singh also had the will; he has a history of volunteerism. He is on the Faculty of Art Advisory Council at York University in Toronto. Since 2007, he has acted as a judge for the Guyana Awards, given annually for business excellence, media and culture, special achievement, lifetime achievement and leadership. The program also awards eight scholarships each year to needy students entering university.

So, a trip to Haiti in its time of need seemed only appropriate.

Originally, he had planned a business trip to Haiti, arriving January 9. But, because of delays with a shipment, he had abandoned that visit. After the earthquake, Singh decided to make a new date with Haiti, especially when one of his clients provided 2,000 tents for the homeless. Since flying directly into Haiti was impossible, Singh chartered a cargo airplane at his own expense and flew the tents into the Dominican Republic, which shares the island of Hispaniola with Haiti, then transported the tents by truck to Port-au-Prince.

He arrived during the immediate aftermath of the earthquake.

Nothing in his past could have prepared Singh for what he encountered; emotionally, he was staggered by the devastation. He found familiar landmarks in ruins: the port was destroyed; there was rubble where streets used to be; the Montana Hotel — "where we stayed for years" — was gone. The Montana had long served as a home away from home for travelling businesspeople, government workers and diplomats who would gather at night in the News Bar to enjoy rum drinks and review the day's events. It, too, was a pile of rubble.

"You are accustomed to staying in a hotel," Singh adds, "but there's no place to stay."

He also worried about the fate of business associates and friends at the Canadian Embassy who were missing, and experienced both hope for their survival and acceptance of their deaths. There was no escaping thoughts of death — the stench of death was everywhere, as were the sounds of crying and wailing.

"The magnitude of this devastation puts you in mind of a biblical scene," Singh says. "Maybe this is what hell is all about."

But in some ways these traumas paled when faced with Haitians who had survived the quake but were fighting desperately against hunger and thirst. "Did you bring water? Did you bring food?" locals asked him. "People were starving," Singh says, "trying any pool of water that they could find."

Singh didn't allow himself the luxury of grief or despair. He stayed focused on the task at hand, on helping whom he could. "It's a forced sense of optimism," he recalls. "You are forcing yourself into optimism."

Singh's experience was heart-wrenching but it served to deepen his commitment to humanitarian aid to Haiti. He continues to provide assistance in concert with charitable organizations. "This is a continuing need and this need is not going to go away," he says. "Haiti is going to go off the radar screen. Once it is off the radar, people will forget that Haiti is there."

Atlas Cargo — free of charge — transports containers bearing supplies to a port of embarkation in Canada, loads the containers onto airplanes or ships and arranges the documentation and other formalities. Charitable organizations obtain the supplies and handle the costs of the containers.

Singh figures the response will continue indefinitely "It's not a situation you can forget," he says. "Once you close your eyes, it comes back to you so vividly."

—◁o▷—

Dr. Aslam Daud and Humanity First Canada's medical team arrived in Port-au-Prince twenty days after the quake, but Daud faced much the same circumstances and had much the same reactions as Singh. Because of the enormity of the challenge, very little had changed.

"It made my heart wrench," Daud recalls. "What I saw was extremely disturbing — that so many people were just out in the streets without homes, without food."

He remembers the wrecked buildings and roads — even a crushed leg dangling out of a window.

Daud is a health-care information analyst living in Maple, Ontario, just north of Toronto. He received his Bachelor of Medicine and Surgery from Dow Medical College, University of Karachi, Pakistan, in 1986. (That institution has since become independent and is now known as Dow University of Health Sciences.) He came to Canada in 1990 and in 2004 became a founding member of Humanity First Canada, the Canadian operation of Humanity First International, a volunteer organization that works to relieve suffering in areas hit by natural disasters and wars.

In some ways, his involvement in Humanity First Canada continues a pattern established during his college days in Pakistan, when he would visit remote camps to organize medical clinics. As chairman of the Canadian operation, he works with others to recruit volunteers and raise funds, but it was in his capacity as coordinator of disaster responses that he went to Haiti.

So, in late January, the Humanity First Canada team of doctors and nurses arrived in Port-au-Prince to set up a clinic. Over the next weeks, the team typically treated 150 to 200 patients a day in the clinic. The conditions and the work took its toll on individuals in different ways, Daud says: "You cannot just continue seeing patients non-stop. You get exhausted; you need to take a break. And when you do take a break, you feel guilty that there are patients who are waiting for you."

Even some of the experienced medical personnel had trouble coping with the tragedies that they encountered in Port-au-Prince. One nurse became extremely depressed and needed psychological counselling before returning home. She had felt such misery over the loss of life; she needed to return to her normal life and surroundings.

Another member of a team returning home had become so distraught at witnessing families that had lost a child, father or mother, that she needed to be with her own family immediately. "All I wanted to do was to see my children and give them a good hug," she told Daud.

For his part, Daud found solace in prayer and he saw prayer as his refuge. "That was the thing that gave me the strength or mental tranquility to cope with it," he says. "I asked myself: 'Why did so many people die? Why is a leg still hanging from the roof and nobody there to bury that person?'

"Prayers helped me at least keep my composure."

LEARNED SO FAR

- Lay aside personal concerns and focus on the task at hand.

CHAPTER ELEVEN

Expecting the unexpected:
How Alex Ruff, Robert Girouard, Tom Popyk, Harris Silver and Victor Carvell fought back

Believe in yourself, and in your dream
though impossible things may seem.
Someday, somehow, you'll get through to
the goal you have in view.
Mountains fall and seas divide before
the one who in his stride
Takes a hard road day by day
sweeping obstacles away.
Believe in yourself and in your plan.
Say not 'I cannot' but 'I can'.
The prizes of life we fail to win,
Because we doubt the power within.

— AUTHOR UNKNOWN VIA MAJOR ALEX RUFF

Being on the ground in the midst of an armed conflict requires a special kind of courage. Every day, day after day, you have to expect the unexpected. You have to stay alert to stay alive. And some days, even that doesn't work.

The NATO-led mission in Afghanistan has presented an often deadly challenge to soldiers, news correspondents, independent contractors and aid workers labouring to restore the beleaguered country. As the death toll mounts, it is easy to forget the role that Afghanistan played in defeating the Soviet Bloc and the former Warsaw Pact during the Cold War. In fact, it is easy to forget the Cold War. But Afghanistan's war against the Soviets in the 1980s devastated what had been a thriving country. It left a gaping hole into which the fundamentalist Islamic militia, the Taliban, drove.

Only slowly has the international community fulfilled its promise to help Afghanistan rebuild. Canadian troops arrived in Kabul in 2003 and Kandahar in 2005.

"Afghanistan is locked in a political contest in which two sides are trying to prove to the people which can best govern the nation," says Dr. Lee Windsor, lead author of *Kandahar Tour: The Turning Point in Canada's Afghan Mission* and deputy director of the Gregg Centre for the Study of War and Society at the University of New Brunswick in Fredericton. "For the Afghan government and NATO, winning that struggle requires moving among those people to deliver aid, hear concerns, build infrastructure, restore order and hunt the Taliban. For the Taliban and the drug gangs, winning is a matter of stopping Afghan government and NATO movement.

"Improvised explosive devices (IEDs) set on major arterial roads are their most cost-effective method of doing that," he continues "In response, most NATO and Afghan National Army operations focus on keeping roads open and on tracking down Taliban IED teams. It is a deadly cat and mouse game in which Canadian and Afghan Army Engineers increasingly bear the brunt."

Soldiers Alex Ruff and Robert Girouard can testify to just how deadly that game is; for them, death by IED and suicide bomber has a very personal meaning. For war correspondent Tom Popyk and contractor Harris Silver, IEDs were an ever-present threat that shaped their daily lives in Afghanistan. For aid worker Victor Carvell, it wasn't death by IED that chilled his heart, but the devastated and maimed civilians that came to the hospitals financed, in part, by Canada. It was a daily reminder that the costs of civil war are high — and everybody pays.

◄◊►

Major Alex Ruff had already done two tours with the Canadian Forces in Bosnia before going to Afghanistan in 2007 as company commander of Hotel Company of the Second Battalion The Royal Canadian Regiment Battle Group (2 RCR BG). There were definitely lessons the career soldier had learned in Bosnia in 1999 and again in 2001 — such as how to earn the trust of the local people — that applied to Afghanistan. But, he says, "There was not the threat of being attacked in Bosnia." That was not the case in Afghanistan.

In early 2007, NATO was focusing its offensive on the centre of the Taliban insurgency in Helmand province in southern Afghanistan, some 150 kilometres west of Kandahar. After a relatively quiet winter post-Op MEDUSA, the conflict was heating up when Hotel Company began its tour.

"Mid-February we got ambushed," Ruff says. "That is an experience in itself, when somebody fires on you. The first few times you're very on-edge."

There was certainly more to come. Easter Sunday, April 8, 2007, a Hotel Company combat team was escorting a convoy moving troops and supplies into Helmand. A light armoured vehicle (LAV) carrying ten soldiers was forward, moving into position to be radio rebroadcasters — ensuring communication between the field and Kandahar — when they hit an IED. Six soldiers were killed. Ruff heard the first reference to "vital signs absent" on his radio.

"Your gut falls right out of you," says Ruff. "It was the worst day of my life. Nothing has topped that. Nothing prepares you for something like this."

Yet, in many ways, Ruff had been training to deal with just such an event his whole life. He grew up on a farm in Tara, Ontario (near Owen Sound), 188 kilometres northwest of Toronto on Georgian Bay. He was the eldest of five boys born in six and a half years. It was a rough and ready household, one that framed his outlook on life. "We are all a product of our experiences and the environment we grow up in," he says.

Ruff joined the Canadian Forces in 1993 right out of high school, attending the Royal Military College in Kingston, Ontario, followed by stints at Canadian bases in Petawawa, Ontario, and Gagetown, New Brunswick, as well as attending year-long command and staff courses in

Kingston and Toronto. In 2010, he was posted to the Canadian Special Operating Forces Command in Ottawa overseeing training and doctrine.

As a professional soldier, Ruff has trained to be ready for anything, so although Afghanistan was in some ways a new experience it wasn't an unexpected experience. From basic training right through to high-readiness training, Canada's soldiers know what they are getting into when the "fat hits the fire."

"You expect it," Ruff says. "You just do what you have been trained to do. When you do that, self-confidence builds. You learn every time something happens. Some parts of the plan work, some don't. There is constant adjustment; being flexible and adaptable is really important."

During Hotel Company's approximately six-month tour, it spent the majority of the time in the desert, living out of its vehicles. At night, they would "circle the wagons" with the tanks and LAVs facing outward. "You can see for miles," says Ruff, making them fairly safe from attack. "We were not worried. Every night we moved; we were rarely in one place more than twenty-four hours. It kept the Taliban off balance."

When they were moving, they were always on the lookout for indications of IEDs and suicide bombers. "It can be extremely tiring and stressful," Ruff says. "But after you do it for awhile, you get used to it. You accept it because there is not a whole lot you can do about it. It becomes almost a challenge."

And, although the deaths on Easter Sunday of Pte David Greenslade, 20; Pte Kevin Vincent Kennedy, 20; Sgt Donald Lucas, 31; Cpl Brent Poland, 37; Cpl Christopher Paul Stannix (reservist), 24; and Cpl Aaron E. Williams, 23, may have broken his heart as company commander, it didn't break his spirit.

"As terrible as it was, everybody came together to get through it," Ruff explains. "Over there, when there is a death, soldiers carry on. We all know that is a possibility when we sign on the bottom line."

The "miracle" of that day, he adds, was the survival of the seventh soldier in the back of the LAV3, Cpl Shaun Fevens, who, injured and bleeding, had the presence of mind to tell a nearby soldier how to administer vital first aid.

It was even harder when Hotel Company finished its tour and Ruff returned to Gagetown, where he was stationed. That gave him the chance to speak to some of the families of the dead soldiers and express his condolences. "What do you say?" he asks. "As soldiers, we accepted the risk when we signed on. But it's not what parents, wives, girlfriends and children signed on for; they have to accept it because it is what their loved one wants."

But as tough as it was talking to the families about their lost sons, it had its own rewards. He learned something about the grace with which some families accept death. "The strength and perseverance some of the families showed," he says, "was truly inspirational."

Despite the challenges of his tour in Afghanistan, Ruff has never lost sight of the importance of Canadian Forces participation. At its core, it is all about people — people helping people. And that lent him strength.

"Our soldiers are representative of Canadian society; they believe in everything the average Canadian believes in," he says. "The average Afghan is no different from the average Canadian down on his luck. He just wants to put food on the table for his family, have a safe place for his family to sleep and have opportunities for his children.

"It is all about helping Afghans get on their feet," Ruff adds. "It makes it worthwhile to be doing what we are doing."

◄○►

Robert Girouard started his ten-month tour in Afghanistan in May 2008 as part of the close protection unit and tactical team for the Joint Task Force Commander, the Canadian Forces senior officer in Afghanistan.

"Even travelling place to place," he recalls, "every day, every time you got into a vehicle, there was always a threat. There were no routes that were 100% safe."

Girouard was particularly sensitive to the threat. On November 27, 2006, a suicide bomber had struck a Bison armoured vehicle on the outskirts of Kandahar, killing Chief Warrant Officer Robert Girouard and his driver, Corporal Albert Storm. Regimental sergeant major of the First Battalion The Royal Canadian Regiment Battle Group (1 RCR BG), respected as a leader and revered as a battalion father figure, "Bobby" Girouard, forty-six, was also Rob Girouard's dad.

"I knew where it had happened," says Girouard. "The arches leading into Kandahar City were a pretty famous spot. Almost daily, I went by where it had happened.

"I didn't play it over and over in my head," he adds. "But it hit me the last day of my tour: 'This is the last time I have to drive by this place.'"

But Rob Girouard is nothing if not determined. He admits he is the type of person who can't help but try harder. And try hard he has. Through a tumultuous time, he has learned how to live with the unexpected.

The Girouard family is military through and through. CWO Girouard, a native of New Brunswick, was a career solider who, over the course of twenty-nine years, had served in Germany, Kosovo, Bosnia and, finally, Afghanistan. In fact, Rob Girouard, the oldest of three children, was born in Rheinmunster, Germany, on September 5, 1983. He and his brother joined the Reserves in 2003 and by 2005 had both joined the "Regulars." His brother went to Royal Military College in Kingston, Ontario, with the goal of becoming a pilot. Girouard joined the infantry, like his dad.

In fact, Girouard was preparing to go to Afghanistan in 2006 with 1 RCR BG, the same battalion as his dad, when he got an email from his dad. CWO Girouard and his commanding officer had decided it was not a good idea to have a father and a son together in Afghanistan. The senior Girouard, who was assigned to Battle Group Headquarters, feared he wouldn't be able to concentrate on his duties if he were worrying about his son. The younger Girouard joined the rear party, the part of the battalion that stays behind.

That November the Girouard family received the devastating news of CWO Girouard's death. He was the highest ranking non-commissioned officer to die in Afghanistan at that time. For Rob Girouard it was the beginning of an emotional rollercoaster ride.

"The biggest challenge was staying motivated," says Girouard, who had earlier taken the "Top Candidate" award at the RCR Battle School in Meaford, Ontario. "After Dad was killed, I didn't go back to work until February."

If it was difficult staying motivated, it was equally tough staying balanced emotionally. Twelve days before Girouard left for his May 2008 tour of Afghanistan with the Third Battalion The RCR Battle Group, his son Nikolas was born. Leaving Nick was extremely emotional for Girouard: "I was going overseas and asking myself, 'What are you doing? Why are you doing this?'

"There is a sense of duty," he explains, answering his own question. "It is part of military life; this is how it is supposed to be."

Girouard finished his tour in February 2009. His second son Christopher was born in August and, by the fall of that year, Girouard was an officer cadet, divorced and living in Orillia, Ontario, with his sons while he completes his university education at the Georgian College Campus of Laurentian University. He wants to be an officer in the Canadian Forces because he wants to be a leader. "I want to make a difference in the day-to-day life of a group of soldiers," he says.

Girouard is in a "good spot" now, as he calls it. "I am finally with the person I am supposed to be with," he says, referring to his fiancé Jennifer. "She will be the glue that keeps the family together. It is not the solder that is the glue; if the significant other doesn't accept that responsibility..."

The glue in the senior Girouard family, his mom Jackie, has also joined the military. As her kids left home, she began considering her own career and started the process of joining the Canadian Forces. Her husband's death suspended her plans, but she returned to them in 2008. She graduated from basic training when her oldest son was overseas and is a supply tech at Kingston. Meanwhile Girouard's brother has graduated from RMC, is a second lieutenant and in pilot training. His sister has married an infantry man from the RCR who in the summer of 2010 was doing his tour in Afghanistan.

"That's been a large factor, knowing that people respect what we are doing," Girouard says. "We didn't just tuck our tail and run away. If I chickened out and didn't go over, I was letting them win. They took my dad; they are not going to take my career, my will to fight."

—◄o►—

Vancouver native Tom Popyk knows first hand that sense of immediate threat. In May 2010, the freelance reporter spent four weeks in Afghanistan, embedded with American soldiers and Marines on patrol in Marjah in Helmand province.

"IEDs are a danger for which you can prepare as much as you want," says Popyk. "But it's not foreseeable. If they're a bit lucky you get blown up; if you're a bit lucky you don't get blown up."

Popyk admits that being on patrol put him at more risk than covering the conflict from the relative safety of Kabul, the country's capital. But he is used to taking calculated risks. Popyk has spent a good part of the years between 2003 and 2010 in Iraq and Afghanistan reporting for CBS National Radio, CBC Radio and Television, CTV Television Network, Global Television, Corus Radio, ABC Radio, BBC Wales, Canadian Press and Deutsche Welle, a German network. He has covered the Falluja and Najaf campaigns, Abu Ghraib and was in Baghdad in 2003 when the regime of Saddam Hussein fell. Overall, he has spent six months in Afghanistan.

"The question is always: 'How far do you push it?'" Popyk says. You are in situations in which boundaries are not clearly drawn and results count for everything. "You don't really know that you've pushed it too far until you've pushed it too far."

Popyk turned to covering armed conflicts at the age of thirty-two. He admits he had always been interested in overseas reporting, even in the years when he was building his news credentials reporting for local Canadian television stations and the CTV National News.

But Popyk has not gone blindly into war zones. He has prepared himself the best he can. For starters, he believes in the power of knowledge. He has taken hostile environment courses, which teach how to survive natural disasters as well as war situations, often considered mandatory for foreign correspondents. The London-based Rory Peck Trust — launched in 1995 in memory of Rory Peck, a freelance cameraman who died while filming in Moscow — provides a training fund which enables reporters such as Popyk to undertake hostile environment training before encountering the real thing. "In that sense," he says, "knowledge is power."

It is also important that newcomers learn from people who have experience in covering hostile situations, such as Afghanistan. "It's a statistical fact," Popyk says, "that people who go into war zones and don't have experience are more likely to die than those who have experience."

Information gathering likewise looms large on Popyk's list of strategies, especially in situations that are fluid. He stays in touch with embassies and non-governmental organizations (NGOs); that yields what he calls "ground-level intelligence."

But, in the end, Popyk admits, nothing prepares you for the over-the-top stress that comes from being in a war zone. You come face to face with your ability to handle the unknown. After all, your survival may depend on remaining cool and level-headed, and keeping your ego out of judgements.

It can change a person, sometimes for the better and sometimes for the worse, says Popyk: "You quickly figure out whether you can do it. You don't really know because you don't really know what the reality in the field is until you experience it.

"Some people can and some people can't," he adds. "And you don't know until you're tested."

◄○►

Harris Silver has played a number of roles in Afghanistan since his first visit there in 2004. He has negotiated with mujahedeen fighters, supervised security of election operations and worked in the Poppy Elimination Program. And he acknowledges that he has been tested. And he knows it has changed him.

Silver joined the Canadian Forces in 1989 at the age of twenty-one, and left in 2004 of the age of thirty-five. During his military career, he had been an infantry officer and had been on several operations in remote and hostile areas, including the Balkans and Egypt. He gained experience in reconnaissance as well as rapid deployments and other military operations.

In 2004, when Silver was asked to be a reference for a friend applying for a job with the United Nations in Afghanistan, he decided to apply for a position himself.

Silver's first assignment as a security consultant came in April of that year, when he became a mobile disarmament unit manager for the United

Nations Development Program on Demobilization, Disarmament and Reintegration. For the next ten months, he met with the many leaders of the mujahedeen guerillas to sell them on the advantages of demobilization and disarmament. He would sweeten the deals by advising the fighters on getting jobs through various NGOs and arranging payment in kind by providing items such as clothing, foodstuffs, rice, grain and cooking oil.

"The ironic part is that we would be talking to these guys during the day," he says, "and at night, they would send rockets into where we were staying."

Silver had to learn to do business the Afghan way. There was no coming to the point quickly and getting the job done, as we do in North America. In Afghan transactional culture, he says, "You spend several days talking around things before you get to the actual issue that you want to discuss." This entailed discussing family matters, government and agriculture issues before getting to the point of the meeting.

"So, it was a lot of learning," he says, "a lot of patience."

From March through December of 2005, he worked for the United Nations Office for Project Services as security operations area manager, supervising security of election operations in various regions of Afghanistan, a position that involved dealing with violent crises.

Silver returned in April 2006 and, for the next year, worked as an advisor in the Poppy Elimination Program, a joint operation between the U.S. State Department and the Afghan government aimed at reducing the opium harvest and introducing crop diversification. Not the least of his challenges was dealing with often conflicting agendas of American, British and Canadian officials as they each took their own approach to the problem. "We had the British who weren't in favour of spraying the poppy fields and the Americans who wanted to spray and destroy them," he says. Canadian personnel, on the other hand, misunderstood the approach to the program. "They thought it was drug interdiction, like the American Drug Enforcement Agency," he says, "and we were all about development."

October and November 2009 Silver was back again, supervising safety preparations for observers at the election centers on behalf of Democracy International, an American NGO contracted to monitor and observe polling centres and the electoral process during the run-off national election. The challenger Abdullah Abdullah withdrew from the runoff, however, leaving President Hamid Karzai in power.

In his new job, Silver has retained his connection with troubled areas. As manager of high-risk deployment for English services at the Canadian Broadcasting Corp., his responsibilities include assessing the risks of deploying CBC staff to hostile areas and implementing risk-mitigation strategies to support journalists and production units.

He doesn't regret his time spent in Afghanistan. He learned a lot. He is more self-sufficient and better able to improvise solutions in crisis situations. He recalls his first trip to Paktya Province, on the Afghanistan-Pakistan border, in May 2004. "In the Canadian military, you knew there was someone to reach back to if you got into trouble," he says, referring to medical support, logistical support and even the administrative support necessary to ensure prompt payment of salaries.

In Afghanistan, as an independent contractor, that didn't exist. Salary payments could fall several months behind. "It's not as if you can go to a bank machine," he adds. Dealing with that shortfall meant going out to the military bases in the desert to ask for help.

Some threats, he admits, you cannot avoid. "The last time I was in Afghanistan," he says, "the biggest threat was being caught in a suicide bombing." You can avoid danger by travelling simply in unmarked vehicles in small security details, by varying schedules and taking different routes, by using radio check-in procedures and avoiding closeness to military or police convoys. But there is no getting away from being in the wrong spot at the wrong time.

"Now, probably, very little bothers me," Silver says. He has come to a space where he distinguishes which of life's problems have solutions and which do not — and he has the capacity to act on the former and accept the latter.

"If there's nothing you can do," he adds, "then why worry about it."

—◦—

Victor Carvell has seen another side of the conflict in Afghanistan. As a member of the Canadian International Development Agency (CIDA) dealing with Afghanistan issues from 1996 to 2009, he has seen the civilian face of civil war — the children without limbs, the widows trying to feed what is left of their families, the old men befuddled by tragedy.

But he has learned to stay focused on the task at hand by emphasizing the positive, by remembering that Canada's actions in Afghanistan have made a difference.

An economist by training, Carvell has seen more than his share of tragedy and turmoil in many of the world's trouble spots. A native of Vancouver, he joined CIDA in 1980, working in a planning capacity in CIDA's operations in Sri Lanka. From 1984 to 1987, he was a field representative for CIDA in Bangladesh. Then, from 1987 to 1990, he was head of programming for East Africa and The Horn, followed by a three-year stint as field director for Egypt.

In 1996, his involvement with Afghanistan began. Based in northern Pakistan in Islamabad, the country's capital, Carvell spent four years as field director in CIDA's Afghanistan and Pakistan operation. His responsibilities included overseeing a program that provided food and other aid to the escalating number of widows and children in need of help in Kabul and the surrounding area. CIDA also financed hospitals in Afghanistan; he made regular visits to those hospitals and witnessed the human wreckage of war.

"We helped to finance the hospitals so I went to see how the treatments were being done," he says. "That was a really challenging experience.

"There were shepherd children who had lost limbs," he recalls, crippled by land mines. "But then you watch them being put back together again."

It was the putting back together again that held Carvell together emotionally. One hospital in particular, run by the International Red Cross in Kabul, tended to wounded shepherd children and adults. This salvaging of human beings was an emotional experience that helped Carvell cope with the affects of war. "It helped me to understand that these folks were getting treatment," he says, "as a result of Canada's financial participation." Because of that, he could watch patients learning to walk again in the hospital's exercise yards.

During this time, Carvell also spent a year as chair of the Afghan Support Group, a donors' council which was the primary connection between NGOs dispensing aid in Afghanistan and the Taliban. Although, Carvell says, there are "un-nice things" you can say about the Taliban, the people with whom he dealt were straightforward when approached profession-ally. "If you cut a deal with the Taliban — which would usually take an awfully long time — it was never reneged on," he says.

At one time, the Taliban had even worked against the opium trade. "They ploughed under much of the opium," he recalls, explaining that they saw opium as contrary to Islamic teachings.

"You always knew that the Taliban were absolutely clean of corruption," he adds, suggesting that the same could not be said for the govern-ment in power at that time in the part of Afghanistan not controlled by the Taliban. Often called the Northern Alliance, that group eventually formed the core of the Hamid Karzai government.

Although Carvell's field role ended in 2000, his involvement in Afghani-stan continued. For the next two years, he was senior policy advisor for Asia at CIDA's Gatineau, Quebec, headquarters. During that time that he was the principal drafter of the memo to the federal Cabinet on Afghani-stan issues after the 9/11 bombings.

Carvell turned his attention to aid issues in Afghanistan once again in 2005, when he spent three years as CIDA's representative to the Canadian mission to the United Nations in Geneva, Switzerland, co-ordinating humanitarian assistance operations globally, including Afghanistan. In 2008-2009, he was director general of CIDA's International Humani-tarian Assistance and Food Aid Division in Gatineau; his responsibilities included food aid to Afghanistan as well as other areas. He retired from CIDA in 2009 and now acts as an occasional consultant for companies specializing in humanitarian assistance and development.

A twenty-six-year career of calibrating and measuring trauma on the ground gave Carvell the experience he needed to deal effectively with stress and human suffering. He sees that experience as an integral requirement when assessing a situation, considering the available options, designing a response and putting it into action.

"You drop into a sense of: what's wrong? how much? how many?" he explains. From there, he says, you form solutions, so that you avoid being overwhelmed by the problems. "It's a mechanism to help you adjust and adapt to a stressful situation.

"Fatalism becomes the flip side of experience," Carvell adds. "You want to ensure that you can use the experience and not just drop into 'Oh god, everybody dies anyway.'"

His experience enabled Carvell to take a pragmatic approach to the horrors he saw in Afghanistan. "In the end, this kind of assistance is primarily about the living," he says. "The dead are beyond you. You're not going to do anything about that; so, you focus on the living."

Carvell took comfort from that fact that he was in a position to accomplish positive results. "If you're with the Government of Canada, you have a lot of resources," Carvell says. Never enough resources, he admits. "But I could make a difference, unlike many who stand around and wish or hope."

The ability to make a positive contribution meant that he got some satisfaction. "That makes you get up the next day," he says, "and go back at it."

LEARNED SO FAR

- When you do what you have been trained to do, self-confidence builds. You learn every time something happens.
- Some parts of the plan work, some don't. You have to be flexible and adaptable.
- Don't let external forces rob you of your will.
- You don't know how you will react in a stressful situation until you are in that situation.
- Some threats you cannot avoid. There is no getting away from being in the wrong spot at the wrong time. If there is nothing you can do, don't worry about it.
- Focus on the living; the dead are beyond you.
- Measure the extent of the crisis and crystallize available choices.

CHAPTER TWELVE

Another door opens:
How Jim Ruta, Glenn Rogers, Connie Smith and Gavin Graham faced losing their jobs and their identities

"When one door closes another opens. But we so often look so long and so regretfully upon the closed door, that we do not see the one which has opened for us."

— ALEXANDER GRAHAM BELL

Losing a job can be a devastating blow. It undermines a person's emotional well-being at the same time as it knocks down the pillars of financial stability. After all, a job not only puts bread on the table but also, for a lot of people, instills a sense of purpose into everyday life. And because we spend so many hours each day at a job, we expect to love what we do. We start to define ourselves and our success in terms of our jobs.

So, when it all comes crashing down around us, it can bury us in doubt. Just ask personal coach Jim Ruta how it felt to be walked to the door by security personnel. Or ask television anchor Connie Smith how one little envelope can wipe out thirty-two years of hard work and promotions. Glenn Rogers' showdown with the boss meant he was shown the door. And Gavin Graham seems to have accepted that, if you live by the sword, you die by the sword. In fact, we might all do well to adopt Graham's view of corporate loyalty.

—◄○►—

When Jim Ruta measures success now, he measures it in terms of how an individual rebounds from personal disaster. And, according to that standard, he counts himself successful.

But in 1997, the Winnipeg native was looking at success from a different angle. A high-powered, highly paid insurance executive, he had all the trappings of success — a six-figure income, a million-dollar home, a Mercedes-Benz, a Porsche. "I had the best of everything," he says.

But he was about to discover how transitory those measures of success can be. His marriage broke down and within a year he was in the midst of acrimonious divorce proceedings, deprived of access to his two children, a ten-year-old daughter and a twelve-year-old son. His health suffered the effects and his blood pressure soared. But that was not the final blow: within months, his high-ticket executive position came to an abrupt end.

It was the perfect storm of personal disasters and it took all the fortitude Ruta, then forty-one years old, could muster to rebuild his life. "All you have left after a crisis is your behaviour during the crisis," he says. "I look back and I did the best I knew how in the best way I knew how. I survived — and I pulled my way through that."

In the late 1990s, Ruta felt he had reached a professional and financial pinnacle. As regional executive manager for Metropolitan Toronto at the Canada Life Assurance Co., he earned about $40,000 monthly and he was responsible for 250 career life insurance agents, fifteen branch managers and fifty administrative staff. "I had arguably the biggest life insurance company organization in the country," he recalls.

He remembers the exact day — Tuesday, February 23, 1998 — and time — 3:23 p.m. — when that ended. "Somebody walked into my office," he recalls, "and said, 'Today is the last day we are going to be working together at Canada Life.'"

Security personnel walked him to the door.

"With that goes a ton of your self-esteem," Ruta says, "your self-identification, who you think you are."

His way of life went out the door as well. He could no longer afford the house, the snazzy cars. All the tangibles he had used to measure his success, to describe to himself who he was and what he had accomplished went up in smoke.

"What do I do now?" he remembers thinking. "I'm not well. My marriage is broken up. And I'm unemployed."

It was a long road back for Ruta. He did receive a financial settlement from his former employer, but it became part of his settlement with his ex-wife. By May, he had found another but less grand insurance position as director of business development, this time with a managing general agency (an insurance wholesaler which acts as a middleman between independent brokers who sell insurance products and insurance companies which underwrite the products). But it lasted only eighteen months; once again he was unemployed and living in a tiny bachelor apartment. He then had a four-month stint with a mutual fund company. Then a potential executive appointment at life insurer Transamerica Life Canada fell through when it merged with another insurer.

"I literally lost three jobs and didn't get one that I was touted to get," Ruta recalls. "I was still working on my blood pressure, trying desperately to figure this out."

He was surviving — very economically — on money borrowed from family and friends. But he was learning — about the value of friends, the necessity of asking for help and putting aside pride in order to survive. "If you think 'I couldn't possibly ask' or 'I can't do this', you're going to be in trouble for a lot longer than you think," Ruta stresses. "I learned that lesson through the depth of that challenge."

One place Ruta looked for help was his religion. His Christian faith has always been important to Ruta but its value crystallized during this time. "I chose to go to my faith rather than a bottle," he says. He credits religious counselling with helping him to keep his balance. His religious advisor, a close friend, knew the intimate details of Ruta's perfect storm and suggested that what had happened was part of God's plan. "And when you're all trained up for it," he told Ruta, "you'll be fine."

After some soul-searching, Ruta accepted the advice of the priest and decided that he had to trust his faith: "I decided 'I can't handle this' and I started to leave things for Him to do, for God to do."

Ruta resolved his employment issue by starting his own company, The Expert Institute, in December 1999. "I'm never going to get fired again. I have had enough of that," he recalls thinking at the time. "The security of the paycheque isn't worth the pain of being pitched out the door." He was determined never again to trust his career and self-esteem to others. "I'm going to be in charge of this now."

Through The Expert Institute, Ruta works with financial advisors helping them "crack the code to prosperity," teaching that success comes from focus, clear communications and dominating the clients' radar. One event that confirmed the direction Ruta had chosen was the invitation in June 2007 to speak on the main platform at the prestigious Million Dollar Roundtable, an annual gathering of some 8,000 top-performing insurance advisors from eighty-one countries, at the Denver Convention Center. Most professional presenters consider an invitation to speak on the main platform a career triumph.

Other aspects of Ruta's life are going better, as well. His health condition has stabilized and he sees his children on a regular basis. And he has learned a lot from his perfect storm. He has renewed his belief in the power of the individual and the importance of believing in yourself. "You have to believe with passion you can get the performance you want," he says. "Ultimately, that's what happened to me."

—◅o▻—

Glenn Rogers, a native of Toronto, spent his career climbing corporate ladders at major Canadian and U.S. media companies. In the 1980s, he was a thirty-something senior executive in the publishing operations of now-defunct Telemedia, and oversaw the trade book operations of another lost stalwart of Canadian publishing, Southam Communications Inc.

By the 1990s, Rogers — a dual citizen of Canada and the U.S. — had moved to the U.S., taking up a senior position at Advanstar Communications. By the time he became executive vice president at publishing and web giant

Reid Elsevier in 1998, he was responsible for four hundred employees and some US$230 million in revenues.

"That was coming from a small newspaper chain in Canada," Rogers says, "to a company with an office in New York and an office in California, going to Oscars and going to the Cannes Film Festival. That probably was professionally the biggest jump."

Still, the position that was his greatest success also brought Rogers his most gut-wrenching experience. A change at the top of Reid Elsevier led to clashes between Rogers and the new CEO. Rogers forgot a basic lesson: it doesn't matter if the new boss doesn't understand the business or wants to change things for the worse, he is still the boss.

By November 2002, those clashes had cost Rogers his job. "So, my greatest professional achievement and greatest challenge came in the same place," he says.

"On reflection, I wasn't surprised," he admits, "I knew the CEO and I weren't getting along."

Rogers's disappointment, however, didn't blind him to new opportunities. Early in 2003, he took a majority position in a small entrepreneurial youth marketing company that was backed by a private equity firm. After a successful exit from that in 2007, he extended his entrepreneurial streak and joined the fifteen employees of Los Angeles-based CarDomain Network, a social network for auto enthusiasts, as CEO and shareholder.

Now, he sees that 2002 firing as beneficial in some ways, as it brought him into the world of entrepreneurship and venture capital, a world he has happily embraced. He wonders if without that push, he would have remained indefinitely in the corporate environment and missed this opportunity to redefine success.

One hurdle through which Rogers had to jump as he made the transition from the corporate to entrepreneurial environment was determining if he had what it took to be an entrepreneur. He did a little soul-searching to assess his strengths and weakness. He knew he didn't want to go back into the corporate environment. "Becoming an entrepreneur was a natural progression," Rogers says, "something I should have done a lot earlier."

For Rogers, success is motivated by fear. "I've always been motivated — rightly or wrongly — by fear," he says. "I think a lot of successful people are. There is that whole idea that you can end up penniless in a trailer park eating cat food.

"If you're driven by that fear, I'm not sure it ever goes away," he adds. "It's always with you. That's just how the world turns for people like me."

◄○►

Connie Smith is one of the most recognizable and engaging personalities on the air and behind the podium in Southern Ontario. From 1976 to 2008, she built her reputation for integrity and compassion anchoring, reporting and producing for Hamilton area television station CHCH-TV.

"I have covered it all," she says about her career, "murders, accidents, interviews with victims of crime. I traveled to New York City and across Canada covering election campaigns and political conventions. But I was always drawn to stories that others didn't want."

Who in the Golden Horseshoe can forget Nipper the Pike, raised by school kids and released into Bronte Creek, or Joe Bananas, the circus chimp impounded at the Niagara border. She connected to her community — and her community loved her for it.

But her career path took a hazardous twist in November 2008 when she was one of a number of CHCH employees who were released from their jobs by the station's owner, the troubled Canwest Global Communications Corp. The nine-month "enforced sabbatical" became a period of reflection and rebuilding for Smith. But rebuild she did. By July 2009 she was back, this time in charge behind the camera as well as in front.

Smith grew up in Burlington, Ontario, not far from Hamilton. Her father is a marine surveyor and her mother a stay-at-home mom who encouraged her daughter to be independent. At Nelson High School, Smith considered becoming an English teacher, maybe an actor. But when she entered a broadcasting course at Mohawk College in Hamilton in 1972, she quickly realized that a career as a news broadcaster would combine performing and educating.

Her first job was in Toronto, on radio station CFRB as the "good news reporter." That led to her first television role at CKVR-TV in Barrie, Ontario, in 1974, where she covered weather and breaking news, then on to CHCH in 1976. So began the struggle to prove herself as a woman journalist — fighting the perception that viewers didn't want to hear a woman read the news, fighting stereotypes that said women couldn't work nights, cover murders or hold her own with a man on the anchor desk.

"The struggle never really ended, just changed," Smith says, "to proving myself as younger women entered the field, and blue-eyed blondes fell out of favour in an increasingly diverse community. Yet, the satisfaction of a job well-done, of connecting with viewers, making a difference, outweighed it all.

"Yes," she adds, "women have come a long way. But, with a few exceptions, the glass ceiling is still there."

In her thirty-two years at CHCH, she piled up the honours. She was named a Hamilton and Halton Woman of the Year, received the Zonta Club of Hamilton II's Founder Award in 2007 and in March 2009 was named a Paul Harris Fellow, Rotary International's top honour for public service. Sertoma Hamilton's Service to Mankind Award followed that same year.

It was a dark day, however, when Smith was handed an envelop by CHCH management that said her services as anchor were no longer required. It hit her hard. "Professionally," she says, "I have never experienced anything like being laid off. I was defined by this job.

"I was stunned," she continues. "I thought, 'I have visited with and interviewed many people who had lost their jobs; now it is my turn.'"

In the months that followed, Smith thought a lot about what she wanted to do. She recalled the events of 9/11; even as the horror of the story unfolded during her eight-hour shift, she found stories of people who needed to do something positive, to make a difference.

A committed community volunteer, Smith also had first-hand experience of people working hard to make a difference. A "St. Joe's Baby," she is a member of St. Joseph's HealthCare Hamilton Board of Trustees and volunteers with Ronald McDonald House, the YMCA Peace Medal program and the Alzheimer's Society of Canada. She is the incoming chair of the Hamilton United Way Campaign for 2011.

Gradually, the notion that people want to do good and be good grew. "Yes, bad news sells," Smith says, "but people are sick of bad news. A good story is a good story — stories are driven by humanity."

Today, Smith hosts and produces, along with her husband Dave, the *Always Good News* show on the CTS-TV system in Burlington. It is the most important thing she has done yet, she says: "These stories will change you. *Always Good News* emphasizes triumph over tragedy, success over adversity, people giving back."

Sometimes, events come full circle. Smith started her career as a "good news" reporter; that's where she has picked up again. And she recognizes the irony in the events that have lead to *Always Good News*: "We think it is the end, only to find that a new opportunity presents itself."

—◦—

Gavin Graham has spent thirty years as a money manager working for large financial institutions around the world. Over the course of his career, he has taken the measure of large corporations and their relationships with their employees. A high-profile commentator on the markets and a familiar face on TV's Business News Network, Graham displays the pragmatism learned over a long career.

"Shall we say," he says, "that the large institution is almost constitutionally incapable of actually acting in a logical manner or following through on all of those management mantras that we have been taught."

Perhaps more to the heart of the matter, although corporations demand loyalty from their employees, in large organizations that loyalty often goes only one way. A hard-working employee can find him- or herself out on the street, regardless of the contribution to the company. Graham calls it going "from hero to zero." But, a person does learn to cope, Graham maintains; he did.

A graduate of Oxford University with a master's in modern history, Graham began his money-management career in England. Money management can be a particularly tough way to earn a living because performance is based on investment returns, and a large part of those returns are based on circumstances beyond the control of the money manager. Take the global economic crisis of 2008-2009. It's an up-and-down business, and a manager can be a star one year, and in the doghouse the next.

That has certainly been Graham's experience. In 1993, for example, he was chief investment officer of the Asian asset-management business of a major multinational bank based in Hong Kong. In 1994, Graham's group was the best-performing money manager in its category; the pension fund for which the group was responsible fell 5% in a year when comparable funds fell by more than 15%. The following year, however, a spike in the value of the Japanese yen caused economic uncertainty and the fund suffered. As did Graham.

"I went from being the hero to zero in about three months," he recalls. "It was a very big reminder that loyalty only runs one way. It was a very useful reminder of the nature of large organizations."

But, Graham says, he had joined the company with his eyes open, knowing it was a highly political organization. He moved on.

In his second most recent incarnation, Graham worked in a Big Five Canadian bank building an asset-management business and, although there were some positive experiences — such as launching an Asian fund in 2003 with a mandate to invest in Asian stocks producing income as well as growth through price appreciation — there were a lot of frustrations.

"When the necessary decisions had to be made, the follow-through or the support was not evident," he recalls. The larger the organization, the more people who become involved in decision making, he adds: "You end up with decision making by committee." That can work against a bold stroke in investing that could earn large amounts of money. "It is almost guaranteed to prevent those organizations from functioning effectively."

Graham, who in 2010 was working with a small Canadian mutual fund company as an investment counsellor, has become very pragmatic. "You come to accept, after two or three experiences, that it is no different — whether the bank or the organization is British or Canadian or American or Swiss or French or Japanese — the same process of politics and internal dynamics means that it's enormously difficult to get anything done in a large organization," he says. "It is directly contradictory to all of the longer-term goals that are talked about at management-leadership conferences."

He argues there is often little justice in the work world and each individual has to take responsibility for his or her own interests, understand the demands of the job and be willing to live with the tradeoffs. It's a case of "Know thyself" and "To thine own self be true."

"It comes down to a very simple equation: you get paid a great deal of money, in which case you should put up with the job that you don't particularly like," he says. That means you accept the long hours, the sacrifice of social life and the extensive travel that your employer demands, in return for the big bucks and the satisfaction that having money brings you.

Or you don't make a lot of money, in which case enjoyment and personal satisfaction become the benchmarks. A position that is truly enjoyable has its own reward, Graham says: "If you love your job, quite frankly it doesn't matter how much you get paid, although you do need enough to keep body and soul together."

In the absence of either genuine satisfaction or a generous salary, you really need to examine your motivations, Graham maintains. If you are not happy in the job, you have to ask yourself 'Why not?' — and why you continue in an unhappy situation. The costs of being unhappy are too high, he adds; we spend far too many of our waking hours at work. And dissatisfaction can lead to alienation, negativity, even marital problems.

"The sooner you're willing to ask yourself that question," he says, "the better."

And Graham is a proponent of being happy in a job. "Quite frankly, if you are unhappy," he adds, "you will not do your job well and the company is not going to be satisfied with your performance." Then, you will find yourself updating your resume and taking the next step.

Certainly, Graham has reached the stage in his career at which he takes his own measure of success. He looks at employment pragmatically: he knows what to expect — such as not expecting loyalty from your corporate employer — and gets on with it, enjoying what he is doing while he is doing it.

LEARNED SO FAR

- All you have left after a crisis is your behaviour during the crisis.
- You have to believe with passion you can get the performance you want.
- Be careful how you measure success.
- You rarely win clashes with your boss.
- People need to do something positive, to make a difference.
- Corporate loyalty often goes only one way.
- By virtue of their size, it is difficult for large organizations to be truly effective and efficient.

CHAPTER THIRTEEN

Listen to your inner voice:
How Scott Bowman, Justin Cooper and Maureen Jensen took the path less travelled

Two roads diverged in a wood, and I —
I took the one less travelled by,
And that has made all the difference.

— ROBERT FROST

Scott Bowman, Justin Cooper and Maureen Jensen have taken different career paths: Bowman and Cooper are both educators while Jensen is a geologist turned capital-markets regulator. But all three have made choices that set them apart from their peers. Bowman's belief in personal responsibility and self-discipline led him to establish a school based on the military model. Cooper's deep Christian faith led to his conviction that young people committed to Christ should be able to get a university education in an environment that is committed to Christ. Jensen chose a profession that was unusual for a woman in the 1970s and, by becoming a regulator, set herself apart from the business world and its drive for profit.

All three have listened to their inner voices and that has taken them down the road less travelled.

—◦—

A vision makes for a precious possession, and no one can accuse Scott Bowman of lacking a vision when he founded Robert Land Academy, Canada's only private military school for grades six through twelve, in 1978. Nor can anyone accuse Bowman — a major in the Canadian Forces reserves until 2000 — of being afraid to swim against the tide when he took as his model the military, with its focus on personal responsibility, organization, teamwork and self-discipline.

"When we started out on this journey," Bowman says, "the whole notion was off the wall and contrary to popular pedagogy. And it remains that way, interestingly enough, thirty years later."

The dominant trend in Ontario schools in the 1970s was liberalization, born out of the recommendations of the Ontario Provincial Committee of Aims and Objectives. Its 1968 report, entitled *Living and Learning* (but more commonly known as the *Hall-Dennis Report*, for its co-chairs the Hon. Mr. Justice E.M. Hall and L.A. Dennis), criticized the regimentation of Ontario schools and classroom practices and recommended education reform.

Liberalization was the furthest thing from Bowman's mind when, at age twenty-seven, he opened Robert Land Academy in Wellandport, Ontario, as a not-for-profit organization with rigorous discipline, academic excellence and physical fitness at its core. A direct descendant of Robert Land, patriarch of one of the founding families of Hamilton, Bowman was educated in the days preceding the *Hall-Dennis Report* and believed in the value of what he calls, "In order for you to get where you want to go, you have to do this!"

Robert Land Academy students — or "recruits," then "cadets" — live by that dictum. Each year, the school takes about 160 boys, who are often considered underachievers; Bowman profiles then as dominant, strong-willed, with a stubborn personality — the kind who will benefit from the highly structured environment of the school. And the school is structured, with remedial tutorials and supervised study halls to enforce academic standards that strive for literacy in language as well as numbers.

The student/teacher ratio is very low. The physical education program includes twenty-three days of training that culminates in a ninety-kilometre march with full pack and which lasts two-and-a-quarter days. School staff, including teachers and military staff, join the march. There are no cellular telephones or televisions on "base" and Bowman believes in competition and the value of sports in which there is a winner and a loser.

"We're a tough school," he admits, "and we make no apologies for it."

Bowman sees the Academy's mandate as three-fold: teach students self-control, provide and ensure a sense of value, and mould good citizens. "Cadets learn to sublimate themselves," he says, "to understand they are one part of something bigger." He believes that sublimation leads to the strong sense of camaraderie that soldiers experience and to taking responsibility for your actions.

Over the course of its thirty-year history, the Academy has graduated some two thousand students and, says Bowman, 100% of graduates who apply to university get their first choice. He estimates that 95% of each year's graduating class apply for university, while others go directly into the army or the Royal Canadian Mounted Police. "So it works," he adds.

But Robert Land Academy has faced its share of controversy and financial challenges. "There was no shortage of folks in some of our established halls of education," says Bowman, "who thought that Robert Land was a rather draconian concept that would peter out and die.

"It's the old dictum," he laughs, "if you stand up and take a position, expect to get shot at."

In its early days some twenty-five years ago, a University of Toronto group criticized the school as too strict. Then, during the mid- to late-1980s, single-gender educational institutions came under attack across the pedagogical spectrum. In 1998, critics blamed the school for the death of two boys who ran away from the school and later died in a train accident in Burlington. However, a full coroner's investigation did not connect the deaths to the school.

As well, the Academy has had various financial issues. The school has only three sources of income: tuition, charitable donations and community fundraisers. Bowman has rejected government funding, for fear it comes with strings attached. But that has made for uneven cash flow. In 1990, the entire staff took a 25% reduction in salary in order to make ends meet. "I have a very complicated financial theory," he says. "You can't spend what you don't have. It's really kind of simple." Besides, "I've always believed that if your product is good enough and has merit the money will follow."

Over the years, Bowman has fielded some large-ticket, buy-out offers. But he has preferred to stay with the Academy. He acknowledges that going against the times will always involve hard choices. "When you're innovating and swimming against the current," he says, "you have to focus very clearly." But in the end, it is your value system that will sustain you.

"That is the crux of it," he says. And Bowman has great faith in his values.

◄○►

Dr. Justin Cooper, too, is of a man of conviction, but he finds his calm in his Christian faith. A noted academic, he stands out because he has lived his faith. And because he has lived his faith, any adversity he has faced has been surmountable, because it is all part of larger plan.

"Be faithful and thorough in your management and completion of the smaller tasks you are given," Cooper likes to say, "and larger tasks will come."

It has certainly seemed that way for Cooper. For thirty years, Cooper has played an ever-increasing role at Redeemer University College in Ancaster, Ontario, not far from Hamilton. His last role was president — he retired in June 2010, after completing his third five-year term — and during that time he saw enrolment grow to more than nine hundred students, steered the university through financial crisis and helped it gain provincial recognition as a degree-granting undergraduate university.

"Your best work is done," Cooper says, "when it is done for a cause you believe in."

And Cooper is passionate about Redeemer. Redeemer is an unusual institution in that it is an undergraduate liberal arts and sciences university that functions within a Christian perspective. Its goal is to provide academic excellence within the context of spiritual growth and commitment to Christ. That principle of higher Christian education in Canada is a cause about which Cooper feels strongly.

"If you do have a deep sense of conviction and passion for something," he says, "some form of external confirmation will be provided to you to give assurance to you."

Cooper came to Redeemer in 1980 as a member of the faculty. A native of Passaic, New Jersey, and a graduate from Trinity Christian College in Chicago, he had a Master of Arts in political science. In 1986, he received a Ph.D. in political science from the University of Toronto — the same year he moved from faculty member to vice president, academic. He became president in 1994.

Cooper admits he did not necessarily seek advancement but opportunity often found him. His willingness to put his back into the job, any job, meant opportunities presented themselves. Although his drive to take great care in his work — regardless of the smallness of the task — may have been founded in a degree of insecurity, it did bring him to the attention of colleagues. "I learned to listen carefully to others, to be conscientious and to be detail-oriented," he says. As a result, he was often asked to take on assignments, sometimes before he was ready. But for Cooper, time spent in deep reflection and prayer was critical to his career decisions.

His first nomination to become president of Redeemer is a case in point. He was vice president, academic, at the time. "On reflection," Cooper says, "I did not feel called to the task, nor did I feel equipped." His lack of conviction was apparent; he did not get the job. But that was not the case in 1994, when he felt ready and full of conviction — fortunately, because his conviction was about to be severely tested.

"It was July 1, 1995. I stood staring out the south window of my office at Redeemer," Cooper recalls, "together with our vice president of finance. We were battling a financial deficit, we had several human resources issues and our student enrolment was falling."

Despite grave concern among his board of directors, Cooper had a sense that resources would appear. "Something would pull us through," he believed. Indeed, an important donor appeared and that crisis was resolved.

It wasn't the only test to his leadership. A few years later, the fear of growth and its fiscal challenges surfaced yet again, with several voices calling for retrenchment. Cooper's passion and conviction carried the day once again.

"If you are called to take something on," he says, "you will be equipped for the task."

But Cooper hadn't been standing idly by, waiting for fortune to smile. He made a conscious decision to reach out to his communities — local, Christian and secular — in the building of Redeemer's presence. For example, he has served on the board and various committees of the Hamilton Chamber of Commerce, and was a board member of the Washington-based Council for Christian Colleges & Universities, an organization of more than one hundred Christian liberal arts institutions. He also developed strong relationships with the provincial government and secular universities through the Association of Universities and Colleges of Canada and Ontario's Postsecondary Education Quality Assessment Board. He learned to use "the languages of contextualization" to bring his dialogue and vision of a Christian university to diverse environments.

"I realized how critical the need for mentorship would be, together with a network of trusted and respected colleagues," Cooper says. "Mentors must be in place long before a crisis arises."

Cooper left Redeemer on firm footing. The university has added programs, including an accredited faculty of education, and expanded its facilities, including additional residences, a library/classroom wing and a soccer complex. Enrolment surpassed nine hundred. And although he is leaving Redeemer he is not leaving the cause of Christian education. He is the executive director of the Council of Christian Higher Education Canada, an organization of thirty-four member institutions, and is part-time executive director of the ten-member Association of Reformed Institutions of Higher Education.

Passion for a cause and prayer and reflection have gone hand in hand for Cooper. Living his faith has meant giving his faith life.

◄○►

Maureen Jensen has never been afraid to take the road less travelled. In many ways, she has made a career of unconventional choices, from becoming a mining geologist when few women were to leaving behind the corporate life to become a regulator in the capital markets environment.

But for her, they didn't seem to be unusual choices. She was only following her "inner voice."

Originally from Winnipeg, Jensen, the daughter of a mining engineer, grew up in mining towns. She came to University of Toronto in 1975 to study geology, graduated four years later with a Bachelor of Science and began her career as an exploration geologist, traveling the world working for small exploration companies and "grabbing knowledge." A registered professional geoscientist, she hit her stride in September 1986, when she joined Noble Peak Resources Ltd., a small exploration company with properties in northern Quebec, Utah and the Northwest Territories.

Although Jensen loved the technical positions and working out in the field, it was at Noble Peak that she started taking on more of a management role. "People kept asking me: 'What would you do in a situation like this?'" she says. She discovered she liked telling them and that she was actually good at management. She found herself drawn into planning activities and, when she was made exploration manager, she led the team that developed Noble Peak's strategic vision. Among her many mentors was the company president.

Jensen's management training escalated exponentially when the founder and CEO of Noble Peak died suddenly from a massive coronary. It fell to Jensen to lead the publicly traded company. "While my colleagues and I were in the midst of grief over the founder's death," she explains, "I had to get to business, focusing on the operation of the company, its balance sheet, the share price, the investment-research community and the needs of staff."

But the mining and exploration community is a close one. Jensen took solace from the many personal and company friends who reached out to help and offer advice during this time.

Jensen spent the last seven years of her tenure at Noble Peak as president and CEO, leaving in 1998.

That is when Jensen decided to test the waters in a different pond. She traded the corporate world for the regulatory world. "I asked myself: 'Is this all there is?'" she says. Obviously not, because she joined the Toronto

Stock Exchange (TSE) and became an important voice in the team that was developing disclosure standards for mining companies listing on Canadian exchanges.

"Of the sixty–six recommendations made by the Mining Standards Task Force at the TSE, sixty-two have been enacted," Jensen says. "Canada now has the best disclosure standards for mining and exploration results in the world."

In 2002, she joined Regulation Services Inc. (RS), the newly former independent market regulator responsible for surveillance of trading on the TSE, as vice president, then became president in 2007, just before RS merged with the Investment Dealers Association of Canada to form the Investment Industry Regulatory Organization of Canada (IIROC). IIROC is the national self-regulatory organization (SRO) which oversees all investment dealers and trading activity on debt and equity market-places in Canada. In 2008, she became IIROC's senior vice president of surveillance and compliance.

Jensen enjoys working in an environment in which she is tasked to uphold the public trust. "It feels like we are doing something important," she says. "We are trying to do what's right and it is important that someone take a stand!

"People think that regulation is boring and bureaucratic," she adds. "It isn't. You join an organization staffed by smart, good people who want to make a difference; they are on the leading edge of change."

Whether in mining or in capital markets, Jensen could be seen as a fish out of water — a woman in fields that have predominantly been a man's domain. But it hasn't deterred her. As a woman leading a mining company, she discovered the only strategy was to "just try and be really good." As a regulator, she says, "I try and address the issues head-on. I have focused on the empowerment of my staff and have followed through with delegation of responsibilities."

A wife and mother, Jensen also serves on the board of Trillium Health Centre where she is deeply involved in policies that she hopes will have significant impact on the quality of health-care. She is also very active in the capital markets industry including membership in the Intermarket Surveillance Group, an association of fifty-one exchanges and SROs around the world devoted to sharing and promoting high market-surveillance standards in the world's markets.

She is proud of her career. It has taken her to where she was meant to go. "Never compromise your ethics," she advises. "Listen to your inner voice and it will guide you, even on what might appear to be small or trivial matters. And always tell the truth."

LEARNED SO FAR

- If you stand up and take a position, expect to get shot at.
- Your best work is done when it is done for a cause in which you believe.
- Listen carefully to others; be conscientious and detail-oriented.
- Never compromise your ethics.
- Listen to your inner voice and it will guide you.

CHAPTER FOURTEEN

Finding fulfillment:
How Yaser Haddara
and Nick Bontis
live according to their values

"We have to listen to each other. We must be focused on the principle of freedom of speech and on the need for forgiveness. We must find a place for dialogue and relationship — then build on that."

— DR. YASER HADDARA

Dr. Yaser Haddara and Dr. Nick Bontis are both associate professors at McMaster University in Hamilton, Ontario. They have very different histories and very different goals. Yet, they both try to live their lives consistent with their personal values. While Bontis's values revolve around hard work and family, Haddara's values extend to his community and finding a way to live within that community in harmony and understanding. So, when Haddara was tested, he looked to those values for guidance.

◄○►

Dr. Yaser Haddara knows what it means to have his values tested. Now a tenured professor in the Engineering Faculty at McMaster University, he had to stand up to university officialdom to realize that dream. On a religious level, too, as a Muslim he has found himself facing conflict and disagreement. By listening and being true to his values, he has learned to deal with those conflicts, as well.

It all revolves around values — knowing what your values are and, he says, "striving for personal fulfillment on the basis of those values."

Haddara was born in Berkeley, California. The son of two academics, he had a peripatetic youth, spending his childhood in Egypt, his teen years in Kuwait and his undergraduate years in St. John's, Newfoundland. He graduated from Memorial University in 1991 with an engineering degree, and then returned to California to do a master's and Ph.D. in electrical engineering at Stanford University, graduating in 1997. After post-doctoral research in Florida and a few industry jobs, he joined the Engineering Faculty at McMaster in 2002 as assistant professor.

In the world of academia, a young professor such as Haddara would be given a three-year contract as an assistant professor. Generally, a second three-year term would follow and, somewhere around year six, the professor would be considered for tenure based on his or her performance as an assistant professor.

The decision to grant tenure is based on three things: research, teaching and service. Under research, the professor must show he or she has developed a body of scholarly knowledge, as evidenced by the receipt of external research funding, the publishing of peer-reviewed articles in recognized academic journals and invitations to make presentations at conferences. Proving effective teaching at both undergraduate and graduate levels requires high student evaluations and peer reviews. Service refers to contribution of service to the university, community and, when appropriate, one's profession.

At the end of that non-tenured period, a dossier of achievement in all three areas is assembled, external references are sought and a three-stage process of review begins. First is a departmental review, then comes the faculty review and, finally, the senate of the university reviews the appointment. To receive tenure and be promoted to associate professor, the assistant professor requires a positive vote by a majority of committee members at each of the three stages.

On the surface, it appeared Haddara had a good record when it came time for him to be considered for tenure in 2007. He could list published articles and had twice received a Student Union Teaching Award. On the service front, he was — and is — an active contributor to the university community, including the President's Advisory Committee on Building an Inclusive Community, and to the broader community, including serving on the board of the Muslim Association of Canada, on the Advisory Committee for Diversity to the Hamilton Chief of Police and on the board of the Settlement and Integration Services Organization.

But these elements did not guarantee a smooth ride for Haddara. His case for tenure and promotion was denied at his departmental level, at the faculty level and, on first pass, by the senate committee. When he was given the full report of the faculty committee, which detailed the comments made against him, he discovered that promotion can turn on the way cases are presented and discussed. Although the faculty considered both his research and teaching good, he faced comments such as "unreasonable estimates of research" and "teaching evaluations are good but downward" and, finally, "poor in administrative duties."

Haddara was chagrined by the way particular weaknesses were exhumed in order to provide a means by which his record could be questioned. For example, like many of his colleagues, he had time-management issues, particularly when it came to submitting grades on time. In the review process, that became proof of his poor administrative skills.

"When you leave something for people," he says now, such as his acknowledgement of poor time-management skills, "you risk that they will misuse that information." You must take care in providing perspective to others, he adds, when those others may be in judgment of you.

It wasn't the end of the matter, however. When the senate committee votes against granting tenure, it invites the candidate to an interview. Haddara prepared to respond, point by point, to each critical element and provide the committee with a counter-perspective. But it was never required. The senate committee asked only two questions, which were enough for it to decide to grant him tenure. He received tenure and was promoted to associate professor as of July 1, 2008.

Haddara still believes some of the comments were unreasonable, even pernicious, but he bears none of his assessors any ill will. "We must be willing to move on," he says.

Although the conclusion was good for Haddara, the process was difficult. He admits that during this time, a crisis mentality developed and he began to doubt himself. When you are under attack, this self-doubt can be crippling, he adds: "You have to believe in what you are doing."

Haddara also took solace from "trusted colleagues." They sometimes provided specific guidance, but most often simply provided grounding and perspective, a mental space in which he could feel safe. Haddara speaks of one mentor with reverence. "When I was in trouble," he says, "he found time for me."

In his broader community work, by virtue of the roles he has assumed in understanding and promoting diversity, Haddara has also found himself facing conflict and disagreement. A spiritual man, he takes strength from his guiding principle of striving for personal fulfillment based on personal values.

"We have to listen to each other," he says. "We must be focused on the principle of freedom of speech and on the need for forgiveness. We must find a place for dialogue and relationship — then build on that."

—◦—

You could call Dr. Nick Bontis effusive, enthusiastic, even irrepressible. He loves his life as an associate professor of strategic management at the DeGroote School of Business at McMaster University, he loves his students, he loves consulting and building innovative businesses, he loves public speaking — but, most of all, he loves his family.

"Family is everything," Bontis maintains.

"I think of myself at twenty-five," he adds. "If I could go back and speak to that guy, I'd tell him: 'Don't worry about all these other things, because family is going to be the Number One priority in your life. Your kids are going to consume you, your wife's going to be a partner and you're going to have a fantastic relationship with your parents, as well as your in-laws.'"

Granted, the twenty-something Bontis might not have been so keen to listen. In 1991 at the age of twenty-two, he was recruited by the president of CIBC Securities Inc., the fledgling mutual fund arm of Canadian Imperial Bank of Commerce (CIBC). It was an exciting time to be in the financial services industry; the amount of money Canadians would invest in mutual funds was about to grow exponentially. Companies were gearing up; fortunes were being made.

"When you're young, you think you dominate the world," admits Bontis. "When you're in a bank in downtown Toronto, you're living the 'Gordon Gecko' lifestyle. It's a cutthroat world. What I was concentrating on was standing out and working hard."

Hard work is one of the values instilled by his parents. Bontis likes to relate how his father came to Canada from Greece in the mid-1960s with $2 in his pocket. He arrived in Toronto by train, and as he exited Union Station, he couldn't help but notice the Royal York Hotel. He walked across the street and asked the first person he could find — in very broken English — for a job. The rest is family history.

"My father tends to be the Type-A, achievement-oriented, very hungry, aggressive, 'let's go for it' type of personality," says Bontis. Different values came from his mother. "My mother is the nurturing; 'take care of your family, your children and your health because that's the most important thing' type of person. I want to be able to balance both sides of that equation."

In 1994, however, CIBC Securities was losing its allure. The president who had hired and mentored him was retiring. The company was changing. "When you get lost in a big bank," Bontis says, "it can be a crazy place to be."

But while at CIBC, Bontis had been introduced to the concept of "intellectual capital" through an article in *Fortune* magazine called "Brain Power: Your Company's Most Valuable Asset." CIBC was one of the two companies featured in the article as putting valuation on human capital.

"Everybody gets the idea that the most important aspect of a business is its people, but we don't really know what that value is," he says. "When a critical employee leaves a business, the financial performance of that business actually goes up, because it doesn't have to pay that salary. We're treated like expenses, when, in fact, we're assets. When a critical employee leaves a business, intellectual capital leaves with him or her, so the value of the business should go down."

It was this "conundrum of intellectual capital" that got Bontis's creative juices flowing. He decided it was an opportune time to go to the Ivey School of Business at the University of Western Ontario in London, Ontario, and pursue a Ph.D. "I was very passionate about learning about this topic," he says, thinking it would help him in his investment career. Instead, he got waylaid by academia; he joined McMaster in 1998.

Needless to say, Bontis is a passionate academic. He approaches the three elements of academic life — teaching, research and service — with gusto. He is DeGroote's first faculty member to receive simultaneously the outstanding undergraduate business school professor award, the outstanding MBA professor award, the President's award of excellence in instruction and the faculty researcher of the year award. Outside the walls of academia, he is on the executive of a start-up mutual fund company, Harvest Portfolios Group, and he has a software company and a consulting company, which provides access to interesting research projects.

"My consulting company was engaged in a project in 2001 with the United Nations," says Bontis, who by that point, was gaining a global reputation in intellectual capital. "The UN asked me to develop a national intellectual capital index, in other words, a comprehensive measure by which countries can compare themselves with each other." His research took him to Jordan and Tunisia post-9/11.

"I met fantastic people, and the project was a fantastic success for the UN," he adds. "I published a great paper out of it, too, from an academic perspective."

Bontis is also the director of McMaster's undergraduate Commerce program, an assignment he takes very seriously. Undergraduates can struggle with a number of issues — medical, psychological, deaths in the family, drug and alcohol addiction — and the goal of Bonits's commitment is to offer career, academic and life counseling. "I find myself many times in the middle of the night thinking about a student I counseled that day, and how I possibly didn't give him or her the best response. It's both a challenge and a reward."

Sometimes students drop out to deal with these critical issues. Bontis is always thrilled to see them return and finish their degrees. "At Convocation, I'll announce their names and they'll proudly walk across the stage to receive their degrees. It's such a great feeling because you know that you had a small part in making those parents who are in the audience smile from ear to ear."

Then there are his activities on the home front. In 2010, the father of three coached the soccer teams of his two sons, ages seven and six, as well as his four-year-old daughter. He also coaches basketball. Last year, in recognition of this coaching and volunteerism, Bontis ran in the Vancouver 2010 Olympics Torch Relay. And he looks forward to continuing his coaching into his kids' teen-aged years. "I definitely want to be there for them as a coach," he says. "I love it and it's a great way to give back.

"The interesting thing again, about the teacher in me, is that whether teaching students or executives or six-year-olds on the soccer field, I love it," he adds.

At the core of his life is his family — what Bontis calls his "big, fat Greek family." Every summer, Bontis's entire family, including his in-laws, go to Greece. He realizes it is a luxury, but it is something he cherishes. "You just have to be part of that big Greek family to understand what it means to take that time. You have to be very, very proactive in taking that family time," he emphasizes, "because it's taken for granted. When something happens to your family, then it's too late."

LEARNED SO FAR

- Believe in what you are doing.
- Know what your values are and live by them.
- Listen to each other.
- Do what you love.
- Take family time. When something happens, it is too late.

CHAPTER FIFTEEN

The price of responsibility:
The entrepreneurial experiences of Greg Cochrane, Jim Letwin and Andrew Alexander

"There is a single reason why ninety-nine out of one hundred average businessmen never become leaders. That is their unwillingness to pay the price of responsibility. By the price of responsibility I mean hard-driving, continual work ... the courage to make decisions, to stand the gaff ... the scourging honesty of never fooling yourself about yourself."
— OWEN D. YOUNG, FOUNDER OF RADIO CORPORATION OF AMERICA

Gregory Cochrane, Jim Letwin and Andrew Alexander are that special breed of businessperson — entrepreneurs. They all traded the financial security of a large organization for the thrills and chills of building and running their own businesses. They risked capital; they risked peace of mind. At some point in their entrepreneurial careers, they suffered setbacks and doubt. Yet, belief in their goals, even fear, something kept them going.

—◦—

This quote by Owen Young is among Gregory Cochrane's favourites. At the age of twenty-nine, this Montrealer turned his back on a regular paycheque and a corner office at an international conglomerate and set his sights on running his own company. And while he did — in time — scale the heights of success, it wasn't before he had slugged his way through the depths.

"Nothing prepares you for being an entrepreneur," admits Cochrane, thirty years later. "I know of no school, no formula, no secrets for being on your own."

But Cochrane didn't fully grasp that in 1981. After all, he had completed a Bachelor of Business Administration from Bishop's University in Lennoxville, Quebec, then a Master of Business Administration from Queen's University in Kingston, Ontario, in 1974. He had progressed steadily in his career, tackling marketing and product management roles, first with General Electric Co. in Toronto, then S.C. Johnson & Son, Inc. in Brantford, Ontario. And he had always exhibited an entrepreneurial bent. "I used to run several little money schemes," says Cochrane, "charging kids to race on my car set, or running a bus service from Lennoxville to Montreal in undergrad."

So, Cochrane can be forgiven for thinking he knew what he was getting into when he borrowed $48,000 from his father to buy a third interest in event management and marketing company, Mariposa Communications and Promotions in Toronto.

Within a year, however, Cochrane's dream was a wisp in the wind. Mariposa was on the verge of bankruptcy and Cochrane found himself enrolled in the School of Hard Knocks.

"Despite all my schooling, and working for GE and S.C. Johnson, nothing could prepare me for my first payroll on my own," Cochrane says. "Or sitting in the lobby begging a large client to pay in full my invoice without me ever starting the project!

"We needed the money," he recalls, "to pay suppliers who wouldn't release the materials we needed to do the job for the client!"

Why didn't Cochrane throw in the towel there and then? What kept him — and his two partners — fighting for survival? "Fear of failure," Cochrane says. "That is one of the driving, underlying motivations of all entrepreneurs. Entrepreneurs put themselves out there —they'll do whatever it takes to succeed.

"Failure," he adds, "is admitting that you're wrong."

So, Cochrane turned to a mantra that many people facing a wide range of crises employ: taking it one day at a time. "We just decided that if we could be in business for just one more day," he says, "we might make it."

Make it they did. The company recovered and Cochrane learned more than a few things about running his own company. One, it's all about revenue, cash flow and gross margin. "How many great businesses failed or never started because they just ran out of capital?" he asks. "And why? Because they were focused on the wrong drivers of the business."

Second, he realized he needed a "numbers person" upon whom he could rely completely. He recruited Paul Luksha ("Lucky," as Cochrane calls him) from S.C. Johnson in 1983; they have been partners ever since.

Third, there are many people who want you to fail. It's not just about taking pleasure in another's misfortune, it's also about jealousy and envy. Cochrane had to keep his personal goals firmly in mind and not be side-tracked by the naysayers.

Finally, Cochrane discovered that running his own company meant he had to work longer and harder than he ever had as an employee. As a provider of event management, marketing and communications services targeting major corporations, his job was not only to sell but also to deliver. As a result, he submerged himself in the needs of his customers. He would routinely begin work at 4:00 a.m. drafting scripts, so that he could meet with a key client at 7:00 a.m.

There is a second part to that Owen Young quote cited earlier that gave Cochrane consolation and inspiration: "You travel the road to leadership heavily laden. While the nine- to five-o'clock worker takes his ease, you are 'toiling upward through the night.' Laboriously you extend your mental frontiers. Any new effort, the psychologists say, wears a new groove in the brain. And the grooves that lead to the heights are not made between nine and five. They are burned in by midnight oil."

It paid off. The company that survived the hard times became an industry leader with typically long-term relationships with major clients such as Canadian Imperial Bank of Commerce, General Motors Corp.,

Glaxo-Wellcome (now GlaxoSmithKline Inc.), Investors Group Inc., Kraft General Foods, Rogers Communications Inc. and Royal Bank of Canada. Embedded deep in Mariposa's "DNA" was a complete and intense focus on its customers, channeled through a caring and intimate relationship that stretched from the CEO's office to the loading dock. Cochrane required the employees of his business (and of later companies in which he invested) to behave as stewards; he, as CEO, knew that he must lead by example.

By 1997, when Cochrane and Luksha — Mariposa's two remaining partners — were approached by Mosaic Group, Mariposa managed more than one hundred events a year and had one hundred full-time employees. It was also highly profitable, with a growing collection of business units offering a wide range of corporate communications services, including electronic technologies, to its blue-chip client list.

They decided to sell. "Mosaic was the right fit," Cochrane says. "We knew the principals; we liked the vision; and, we liked the cash."

There was also a sense it was time. Businesses that rely on creativity are not that "scaleable" and it is hard to "mass-produce" processes.

That was by no means the end of Cochrane's entrepreneurial career. A self-confessed "serial entrepreneur" who "backs the person, not the numbers," Cochrane continues to be busy both in business as a venture capitalist and in his chosen areas of philanthropy, including a role as an active alumnus of Queen's University.

He is also a committed mentor. "I believe young people should look to have mentors," he says. "Time and talent are two luxuries that can be given freely! It's so important for us to give to those who want to step into the ring. They must learn that no matter how brilliant or unique their idea or business is, it all starts with hard work."

If you plan to travel the entrepreneurs' road, he advises, "Focus on the immediate with an eye to the future."

What, exactly, does that entail? Here are Cochrane's pointers:

a) Recognize what you are good at. What is your highest purpose?

b) Keep daily/weekly/monthly goals. Celebrate wins; congratulate yourself when the day is done. Reflect on what can be done better.

c) Set a three-year personal plan. Thirty-six months is plannable. Set personal and business goals at the same time. Recognize that there is no work/life balance as an entrepreneur.

d) Remember, goals are dreams with deadlines.

e) Share the wealth. Don't go it alone; you can't do all things. If you trust a person with skills that are complimentary, go into it together. Cochrane and Luksha have worked together for thirty-three years.

◄○►

Jim Letwin calls it his "jump to light speed." That is the time in 1986 when he risked his capital and his livelihood and leapt into the uncharted waters of entrepreneurship. Not only did he abandon the regular salary and substantial resources of the corporate environment, but he also sold his family home to raise capital to invest in the small business he was joining.

"There was a poignant moment," recalls Letwin, then thirty-one. "The moving firm had jammed all the stuff from our three-bedroom house in the country into its truck. The truck was backing up to unload all this stuff into our small, rental home in Brantford [Ontario]. When the truck door opened, it revealed my wife standing on the porch, fighting back the tears."

It was what Letwin calls a "moment of truth," one of those times when it becomes clear what you are really made of. "That's when it gets personal," he says, "when you put your own money into a business and it affects your family."

Fortunately, it has worked out well for Letwin. He is now the president and CEO of JAN Kelley Marketing, a marketing communications agency based in Burlington, Ontario, that — thanks to his drive and "a great team" — has grown to fifty-five employees and a healthy roster of clients. His wife's faith in him has been rewarded and their children have grown into young adults who do him proud.

Yet, it wasn't an easy transition. "When we moved into that rental house in Brantford," Letwin recalls, "I was a frustrated person, angry at myself. I couldn't believe what I had maneuvered my family into."

He has definitely learned a few lessons since then — about small business, about himself, about the value of family and about passing his knowledge along to the next generation.

A farm boy from Sherkston, Ontario, in the Niagara Peninsula, Letwin's formal education began with an undergraduate degree in biology from McMaster University in Hamilton, Ontario, in 1978. In 1980, he added an MBA from the University of Windsor in Windsor, Ontario, and started on a life of marketing. He had found his calling. Letwin went to work for Ralston Purina Co. in Mississauga, Ontario, as an assistant brand manager.

"I was intensely interested in the discipline a large corporation brought," Letwin explains. "I always fancied myself as someone who, through disciplined thought, could find solutions to complex issues."

He believed the corporate environment would show him the way to disciplined thought, to understanding the way business innovators thought. But, when he didn't think he was learning fast enough at Ralston Purina, he moved to Warner-Lambert Co. in March of 1981. "I had it in my head," he says, "that I needed to get to a bigger organization to learn more."

But bigger wasn't better, he admits. Although he wasn't learning what he had set out to learn, he was learning — about the nature of large organizations. "Those Dilbert cartoons are written for a reason," he says. "In large corporations, there can be alienation, a feeling of being remote, that what you are putting your energy and thoughts into doesn't matter as much as the corporation itself."

In the fall of 1983 he moved to S.C. Johnson & Son, Inc. in Brantford. It was better, he says, and he stayed there for almost three years. But, by that time, "I was yearning to have more control over my own destiny," he says. "I wanted to achieve things more in line with my own personal needs and values."

As a brand manager at S.C. Johnson, he did some project work with a small agency, JAN Advertising. He liked the people at JAN, especially Al and Ken Nicholson, and the fourteen-person agency was looking to grow. He made the leap. He exchanged his home for cash to buy into the agency and his corporate digs for a wobbly desk, a pad of paper and a dull pencil.

"What have I done?" he remembers asking himself. He was making less money than he had been and was trying to develop enough new business to pay his salary. "You don't really understand cash flow," he says, "until you don't have cash flow."

But Letwin is resilient. He set to work trying to instill at JAN the marketing discipline that he had learned in the corporate world. This required some adjustment in his thinking. "I tried to take all the systems I had learned at the big corporations and impose them on this small business," he says. "I was trying to turn it into the very thing I had abandoned." Not the best idea, perhaps, but some of those disciplines stuck and paid off.

And help came from an unexpected source. During his time at the University of Windsor, Letwin had been a teaching assistant to the faculty chair of the marketing department, who was a partner in a marketing research firm with another faculty member. Letwin had impressed the prof and his partner in the research firm with his diligence and initiative. When the research partner became general manager of Navistar Canada's parts operations, he called Letwin for help. "If you make a bit of effort people remember," Letwin says.

JAN picked up Navistar Canada as a client, starting with its truck parts marketing business in 1990; it grew to include Navistar's Canadian new truck business in 1993 and eventually the North American truck parts business.

There was one final issue that needed resolving before Letwin could move forward. JAN's share transfer methodology was outdated — he and other minority shareholders were paying for shares with after-tax dollars — and despite Letwin's efforts, he wasn't getting ahead.

"With the jump to light speed, the business was moving so fast," he says, "yet, the money was not following. We believe that if you work hard, you'll get money. But if you labour for too long with no money, you start to wonder if your efforts are worthwhile."

Letwin was certainly having his doubts. But two things happened to reaffirm his value. First, JAN's senior partners rose to his challenge and found a new pricing formula that made the transfer of shares affordable. Second, Letwin started teaching business at Mohawk College in Hamilton.

"There's magic that happened when I started teaching," he says. "'The one who teaches learns the most.' I opened my mind to the energy and power of young people."

He has continued to teach; he now teaches in the MBA program at the DeGroote School of Business at McMaster and he hasn't lost any of his sense of engagement.

In 2001, JAN Marketing merged with Kelley Advertising and moved its headquarters to Burlington. Letwin's experiment in entrepreneurship certainly paid off. He enjoys what he is doing. He has been able to devise the kind of company he wants. "I like to work at a place where the personality of the people infuses into the environment versus the personality of the environment infusing into the people."

He has also articulated the agency's vision in a way that makes it accessible to clients and staff alike. He refers to an Oliver Wendell Holmes quote: "I would not give a fig for simplicity this side of complexity, but I would give my life for simplicity on the far side of complexity."

"That is what we do here," Letwin says. "We create simplicity on the far side of complexity. If you can't communicate with clarity, no one is going to repeat it. If customers are going to be your goodwill ambassadors, employees have to be your disciples."

‹o›

There are many potholes and sharp turns on the road to entrepreneurial success. And a couple of decades of smooth road doesn't mean there aren't detours ahead. Andrew Alexander had compiled a compelling list of accomplishments in Canada and the U.S. since 1974, when, as a twenty-nine-year-old, he bought the Canadian rights to comedy showcase Second City. But it didn't make hitting his roadblock any easier. Comedy may be his forte but there was nothing funny about what happened in 1997.

"It put me behind the 8-ball financially and personally," Alexander recalls. "I was on the hook for a lot of stuff."

Born in London, Eng., raised in Brampton, Ontario, Alexander attended what was then Ryerson Polytechnic Institute in Toronto. After he left

Ryerson in 1967, he held media sales positions, but his passion was comedy. He started producing shows at the Global Village Theatre and took the right turn when he bought Second City in 1974. Productions he orchestrated at the Toronto institution entertained a generation of Torontonians and launched the careers of Gilda Radner, John Candy, Dan Akroyd, Andrea Martin, Catherine O'Hara, Eugene Levy, Martin Short, Joe Flaherty, Mike Myers and others. Alexander sees his biggest success as the SCTV television series which ran from 1976 to 1984 — the first-ever Canadian comedy series sold internationally.

When Alexander and his partner, Len Stuart, bought the USA Second City operation in 1985, they established their entertainment empire. Alexander became chief executive and producer at Second City Inc.

Until 1997, Alexander and Second City added to its list of credits. But the opening of a specially designed facility for Second City operations on Blue Jays Way, just North of Toronto's skydome, gravely overextended the company. The high-end building started sucking up cash; the final straw was the SARs scare of 2003, when tourism in Toronto took a serious nosedive, punching a hole in Second City revenues. Fifty-six Blue Jays Way closed its doors in 2004 and Second City reopened the next year in a smaller space across the street.

"We overbuilt," admits Alexander wryly. "We made some architectural mistakes, design mistakes."

But they weren't the only mistakes. "If I had it to do over again," Alexander says, "I'd probably make the business more efficient and a little more buttoned-down when it comes to the numbers."

But the toughest lessons weren't financial ones. When a major venture blows up, says Alexander, the entrepreneur has to fall back on character-istics that have little to do with finance. He or she has to plumb his or her own inner "wiring" and do some "serious introspection."

"Entrepreneurs are used to setbacks," he says. "It's the nature of that world. You're going to try some things that don't work and some things that do."

What the entrepreneur needs to do — and what Alexander did — is evaluate his or her strengths and weaknesses. When undertaken thoroughly and honestly, he maintains, self-analysis can be a healthy means of improving your ability to deal with others in business situations "What mistakes did I really make here?" Alexander asked himself. "What did I not think through properly? What were the things that contributed to the architectural issues? To partnership issues? What was my role in that?

"Everything is persistence," he says, "getting off the mat and getting back at it. You either get up or you don't. Some people just don't get up."

Alexander did.

LEARNED SO FAR

- Know thyself — or, to repeat Owen Young, have "the scourging honesty of never fooling yourself about yourself."
- Work hard.
- Understand the financials.
- Clearly articulate your company's vision if you want employees and clients to follow you.
- When you're knocked down, get up and get back at it.

CHAPTER SIXTEEN

Your personal brand:
How Susan Caldwell, Steven Kruspe and AnneMarie Ryan parlayed that into a business

"I am a builder, not a maintainer."

— STEVE KRUSPE

Consultants are entrepreneurs of a sort. Like entrepreneurs, Susan Caldwell, Steve Kruspe and AnneMarie Ryan have all forsaken the salary and security of working for large corporations to run their own businesses. But the businesses they run are based on going in and helping clients solve specific problems — then getting out again. Kruspe calls it "the SWAT team" approach. Or, as Caldwell says: "I work directly with the customers and work as a team energized to solve client problems."

But these problem solvers face challenges of their own, and they have had to turn their skills to understanding and learning from those problems.

—◦—

In the mid-1980s, Susan Caldwell traded corporate life for the life of an entrepreneur. She parlayed her love of teaching and learning into Metrix Group, a Toronto-based consulting firm that provides human resources performance and development programs for a wide range of clients, including pharmaceutical, biotech and financial services companies as well as governments.

She made the switch, not because it meant less work, but because it meant less bureaucracy and more autonomy. "There are constraints in corporate life," she says, "that simply weren't going to align with my own needs. Corporate life is as challenging and as much work as being an entrepreneur — but without the benefits.

"As an entrepreneur, you begin to work for your colleagues and your clients," Caldwell adds, "instead of for the people over you. I found that was better for me: to work for my team, rather than for shareholders."

Caldwell's road to success wasn't paved with gold, however. Although she didn't teeter on the edge of financial failure or over expand — like Greg Cochrane and Andrew Alexander in the previous chapter — she had her share of "explosions," lessons retrieved from mistakes and things she wished she had done but hadn't. But she has the entrepreneur's tendency to see the glass half full. She counts herself lucky; in fact, she says, "I'm one of the luckiest people around."

Caldwell didn't set out to be an entrepreneur. Raised in Brockville, in eastern Ontario, she graduated from the University of Toronto in 1974 at age twenty-three, with a Bachelor of Science degree. She followed that with an education degree from Queen's University in Kingston, Ontario, and taught for four years at Hamilton Board of Education. She loved teaching but admits it wasn't where she wanted to end up. She went back to school and did a master's degree in education at Ontario Institute for Studies in Education in Toronto.

In 1981, Caldwell joined accounting and consulting firm Ernst & Young in Toronto as a junior consultant in the educational services group. She moved from there to Royal Trust Co., which has since been swallowed by Royal Bank of Canada, as director of training and development. At both places she admits to working with three outstanding bosses. "I always knew what I could do but I never knew how I could do it," she says. "And

I never knew how well it could be done and how it could be used. Those three senior people had a major impact on my beginnings."

Starting Metrix with business partner Christine Pylat was a chance for Caldwell to put to work what she had learned for her own benefit. It gave her a chance to build her leadership team of five and to understand her value system and how it fit into a business environment. "Anybody coming into consulting has to know him- or herself," she says. "You have to be able to reflect constantly on who you are and make sure that that is never compromised. So, you have to know yourself and know your values."

Caldwell acknowledges that things didn't always go smoothly. And it often wasn't just one thing that went wrong, it was an "explosion" — a key person leaves, a client disappears, computers crash, a key person's child ends up in hospital. "I find that the most challenging times are when many things happen at once," she says. But she takes a pragmatic attitude to such challenges. "It can be dealt with; it can be planned for; it's part of doing business."

Did she make mistakes? Sure, but not exactly mistakes, Caldwell says: "A mistake is something that you cannot recover from. So, to me, if you can recover from it, it's not a mistake. That's really the cost of doing business. In retrospect, you may wish you had done something differently, but you make decisions based on the information you have at the time."

Caldwell does have regrets, one that is fairly common to entrepreneurs. "I wish that I had had a really strong financial partner, someone who could give me really good advice," she says. "What does strategic investing mean in a business? How am I going to invest strategically in this company?

"I knew I needed to invest in people and I needed to invest in processes and tools," she adds, "but I wish I had that strategic-investment mentality the whole way. I could have done more by working with a strong financial strategist."

The other area in which she could have done better, she says, is building a shared vision with her team: "I knew I had to create a vision that was felt by everyone and that our core values were important. But I didn't know how to do that as well as I would have liked. How do you get people to align around a vision, to come to work with their hearts and minds? How do you get their intrinsic sense of self aligned with the corporate vision? Getting the entire team aligned around the vision was critical — and difficult."

The challenge currently facing Caldwell is one facing many small and medium-sized business owners — succession. By 2015, she would like to be in a position to step back from Metrix, yet be assured that the business would continue without her. "Most companies don't survive the original owners," she says, "But I want the business to function on its own. Yet, I want it to be a sustaining presence in my life financially and I would like to be involved strategically. So, I am working with my leadership team to ensure that happens."

Like many entrepreneurs, Caldwell intended to work "forever." So, the feeling that it would soon be the "right time" to step back from the business surprised her. "Even though you say you are going to work your whole life," she says, "there is ultimately a point at which you want to make a change. I wish I had known that because I would have done things a bit differently."

As with strategic investing in her business, she would have planned strategically for her eventual withdrawal from the business.

Caldwell has great plans for how she would like to spend the next decades, and they are extensions of her business life. She would like to be part of a new governing body that would support small and medium-sized businesses and bring to bear the experiences of her twenty-five-plus years as an entrepreneur. She would also like to apply her education consulting skills to making sure every Canadian graduates from secondary school.

"Over the past twenty-five years, we have had terrific customers," concludes Caldwell. "We have always been able to uphold our values. That makes me proud.

"Do what you love, hire good people," she advises, "and you will attract and retain loyal customers."

—◅◦▻—

Steve Kruspe likes the view from ten thousand feet. A principal of Capstream Inc., an Oakville, Ontario-based information-technology consulting firm, he relishes the big picture.

"People, especially IT people, get caught up in small details and lose sight of their objectives," Kruspe says. "It is so important in business, no matter what your business is, to maintain your perspective."

Kruspe has spent the better part of twenty years as an IT consultant — there have been the occasional lapses into full-time employment — bringing that perspective to Canadian wealth-management companies. That kind of "SWAT team" approach of getting in, dealing with the issue and getting out suits him to a T. "I am a builder," he says, "not a maintainer."

A native of Brantford, Ontario, Kruspe attended McMaster University graduating in 1979 with a degree in biochemistry. But, along the way, he did take a few science electives that required he learn a programming language. Then, in his last year, he became interested in business. "I decided to get a job in the business world," he says, "for one year — to see what it was like."

In many ways, he found the ideal opportunity. A small to medium-sized screen-printing business in his hometown hired him on as its IT guy. Kruspe was a one-man show with all the opportunities that entailed. "I had to change my hat every five minutes," he says.

He ran the IT system, modifying code. That made the job interesting enough, but after he was there a few months, the company decided to replace the system. That gave Kruspe the opportunity to think big picture and to learn the lessons that would stick with him throughout his career. "To run the system," he says, "you have to learn the business."

In this case, it meant understanding how the purchasing department worked, how the admin side handled invoicing and payables, how the production side approached workflow. "In the tech-support business," Kruspe says, "tech has to understand how the business works, not just at a superficial level, but *really* understand.

"Another thing it taught me," he continues, "always put yourself in your customers' shoes, whether they are external or internal customers. If you understand how they are going to use the system, you can build it much better."

Those two principles have served Kruspe well. Over the next five years he worked his way east to Toronto and a job in the financial services arena working for investment dealer Nesbitt Thomson Bongard Ltd., a predecessor company to today's BMO Nesbitt Burns Inc. He credits three mentors with teaching him the fundamentals, and the complexities, of the securities business: Aubrey Baillie, Charlie Moses and Ken MacDonald.

In 1990, Kruspe started consulting. "I tried to escape from financial services a couple of times," he jokes, "but I kept getting sucked back in."

In 1997, he was hired by Paul Bates (one of the authors of this book) when Bates started an online discount brokerage, Priority Brokerage Inc. By the time American discount giant Charles Schwab Corp. bought Priority and its sister company, full-service brokerage Porthmeor Securities Inc., in 1999, Kruspe was on staff. "Sometimes, you get lured into full-time from consulting," he explains, "when there is a good marriage and you have been able to road-test the relationship."

Kruspe went back to consulting in 2003, some months after Charles Schwab Canada was bought by Bank of Nova Scotia.

The next siren's song was GMP Capital Inc., a Toronto-based investment dealer that was building a private client or retail business under the leadership of James Werry (now Richardson GMP Ltd.). The challenge for GMP: it wanted to attract advisors who served affluent clients. So, it wanted to present those advisors with a sophisticated technology platform that surpassed other systems. That led to Kruspe and his colleagues developing something truly innovative.

"We combined front office and back office, order management, client relationship management and document management all in one application," says Kruspe. "We tied it all together."

After several months consulting, Kruspe signed on at GMP and stayed put for the next three years. "There is always an element of strategic work," he says, explaining the attraction, "in which important decisions needed to be made." It goes back to his being a "builder" not a "maintainer."

Now, Kruspe spends about 50% of his time working with Recognia, an Ottawa-based company that offers online investment research and analysis products. Recognia came to Kruspe because it wanted to expand; there were opportunities for increased revenue but they carried a big price tag.

"One of the problems with a start-up," Kruspe says, "is lack of focus. When we started consulting in 1990, we were trying to be everything to everybody. It took us three years to recognize that you have to pick your battles and focus on that."

So, Kruspe took Recognia through a similar exercise: "Where do we want to be in five years? What does the product need to look like in five years? What steps do we need to take to deliver new product in the next five years?" They went from big-picture strategy down into short-term tactical.

And that is the pattern Kruspe follows, the view from 10,000 feet, down to ground level. He has never forgotten the lessons learned from his first job and he is happy to share them.

"Learn the business you are in," he advises. "Understand that the scope of your job is broader than just your own job."

–◀◦▶–

AnneMarie Ryan is a focused, determined capital markets consultant who figured out what she is good at, and then got better.

Over the past thirty years, Ryan has ridden the wave of technological change that has engulfed the world of stock trading and stock exchanges. An expert in what makes it all click, she counts herself fortunate to be running her own consulting firm, Toronto-based AMR Associates Inc. But she didn't get there without making sacrifices and accepting tradeoffs. She put in long hours that often compromised her creativity and perspective. But one lesson she learned along the way — never sacrifice your ethics and integrity.

"Whether you work for a company or whether you're a consultant, as you build your career, you're really building your own personal brand," Ryan says. "At the end of the day, what's going to keep you in good stead is establishing the quality of the work you do, understanding your business, and having ethics and integrity."

A graduate of University of Toronto in 1971 with a B.A. in political science and in 1978 with a Master of Business Administration from U of T's Rotman School of Business, Ryan entered the capital markets business just as it was verging on momentous change. In the 1970s, stocks were still bought and sold manually on the trading floor of stock exchanges by floor traders exchanging pieces of paper. Once two traders had made their deal, transactions and resulting prices were posted by hand on one of numerous boards on the exchange floor. It took several days for the trade to "settle" and the money to change hands.

"When I started in this industry in 1972," Ryan explains, "technology was just starting to be used in stock exchanges. I had the good luck and good fortune to work on one of the first automated trading systems, which was the Toronto Stock Exchange. Fast forward thirty-plus years, technology is the entire foundation of the industry. I can't imagine doing any sort of trading without technology."

Over the course of her career, as trading floors were replaced with computers and electronic exchanges, Ryan's expertise grew to cover all phases of processing stock transactions, including trade order management, online trading, exchange and alternative trading systems as well as clearing and settlement systems.

She earned her expertise by working in a number of environments. In the 1990s, she was deeply involved in two start-ups in a row: an online brokerage site, the first to offer access to initial public offerings, and a clearing correspondent brokerage firm. Over the past decade or more, she has worked on a project basis with the provincial securities regulator as it came to terms with the new world of electronic trading. In 1999, Ryan was special advisor to the Ontario Securities Commission (OSC), as it developed policies regarding alternative trading systems in Canada. In 2004, Ryan landed another assignment from the OSC, this time helping develop its concept paper on "best execution" of stock trades. More recently, in the summer of 2010, Ryan went to Australia to measure the impact technology is having on the investment business for the Australia Securities and Investment Commission. She has also worked with mutual fund companies and companies offering electronic trading platforms.

But none of these milestones were reached without tradeoffs. In the case of the start-ups, on the plus side were the people with whom she worked and the relationships she formed. "In both cases," she says, "we were building companies that were challenging the status quo — trying to build new business models and do things better. When you're working so intensely, you really do bond with your co-workers."

But the hours were long. "Earlier in my career, I was very focused on working hard," she explains. "It's a very fast-paced industry; you get so focused on work, you let it drain you, then you're not as creative and you lose your perspective."

Creating AMR Associates in 2002 brought another set of tradeoffs. On the plus side, she was her own boss and got to find the kind of work that interested and challenged her. On the other side of the coin, however: "The whole key to consulting is that you have to get jobs," she says. "You walk away from having a full-time job that pays you a salary. You are taking a risk. But, ultimately, you get to choose the projects that you want and the type of people with whom you want to work. For me, that's been the most rewarding part of consulting."

So, what advice would Ryan give to someone interested in pursuing a career as a consultant? "The most important thing is to establish your credibility," she maintains. "You have to have a network, you have to be recognized, and you have to be known in your industry for having specific types of expertise.

"Second, you need a job that has a profile," she continues, "so people can get to know you and know what you can do. And the third thing, always give back to the industry — speak at conferences, teach seminars. It's important to help others as they build their careers and form their paths."

One way Ryan has given back is by being on the board of Women in Capital Markets (WCM), an organization established fifteen years ago to encourage women to enter capital markets and to promote their advancement. She has been chair of the WCM education and outreach committee, which has taken her into high schools to talk about careers in capital markets. "For the most part, students really don't know a lot about capital markets and how they work," Ryan says. "I find it tremendously rewarding. Whenever I would go and speak to students in a class, I would get as much out of it as they did. They were incredibly energizing."

But in the end, Ryan's three points all circle back to integrity. To make it as a consultant — or just make it — you have to be trustworthy. "If people don't know that you're someone who can both deliver the goods and do it with integrity, then your brand doesn't stand for a lot. Too often people forgo doing the right thing for doing the expedient thing. But in the long run, your ethics and integrity stand beside you for your entire career."

LEARNED SO FAR

- Know yourself and know your values.
- Hire good people.
- Maintain your perspective.
- You can't be everything to everybody. Focus your efforts.
- Put yourself in your customers' shoes.
- Never sacrifice your ethics and integrity.
- In business and in life, pick your battles carefully.

CHAPTER SEVENTEEN

The reward of failure:
How Alex Lowy and Arnie Strub gained perspective

Failure is only the opportunity to begin again, only this time more intelligently.

— HENRY FORD

Both Arnie Strub and Alex Lowy have had to endure watching companies in which they were personally and financially invested struggle for survival. The circumstances were very different and their challenges came at different points in their careers. By the time Lowy worked to rescue the company he had co-founded, he had accumulated enough experience to handle it with perspective. That was something Strub still had to learn. In both cases, however, their experiences reinforced a valuable lesson about the nature of failure and the importance of perspective.

◄○►

Arnie Strub was just finishing his MBA at McMaster University in Hamilton, Ontario, in December 1986 and interviewing for jobs — he had just been called back for a second interview at Xerox Corp. — when his father approached him about entering the family's pickle business.

"Arnie," he said, "if you ever thought you might come into the pickle business, I could use you now."

So, Strub, then twenty-four, joined the business started by his grandfather in 1929. Twenty-two years later, as executive vice president, he was guiding the company though a voluntary restructuring, as the family weighed its options for recapitalizing the company by selling part or all of it. In December 2008, Strub's Pickles was sold.

It was a devastating time. "It is almost like a death in the family," says Strub. "You go through a period of mourning." It also meant the then-forty-six-year-old had to assess his capabilities, weigh his career opportunities and take stock of the lessons learned working in the family business. And, as difficult as it seemed at the time, in retrospect, Strub was well prepared for what the future would hold.

"My feeling had always been I would eventually get into the pickle business," says Strub of that call in 1986. "I just wanted the opportunity to make mistakes with other people's money first."

But a few months earlier, Strub's grandfather and great uncle decided to retire from the business and pass the reins to Strub's father. It was a time of increasing competition in the "refrigerated pickle section" and, although the family had always focused on producing a quality product (his younger brother had already joined the company on the production side), it was weak on the sales marketing side. Clearly, his dad needed help, so Strub joined the pickle business managing the retail sales brokers.

"It was trial by fire," says Strub. "The retail brokers trained me. But anything I did to add value was greatly appreciated because we hadn't been doing that before."

The company was growing quickly. By 2008, sales had quadrupled since 1986. But the company had used debt to fund its expansion, which had added significantly to overhead costs. "It was done for legitimate economic reasons at the time," says Strub, "but we couldn't get rid of the associated debt cost."

By 2008, it had reached crisis proportion. Cash flow was fast becoming an issue. Recapitalizing by selling part of the company was one solution, but, admits Strub, "If you are willing to sell part of the business, you have to be willing to sell all of it." The family also knew that if they couldn't sell the company fast enough, they would have to seek voluntary restructuring with their suppliers.

The task of dealing with suppliers fell to Strub. "We had to ensure supplies kept flowing in," he says, "so we could maintain production and sales."

But how much to tell suppliers was a dilemma for Strub. Nothing he learned at business school prepared him for day-by-day survival during a crisis. Some of the suppliers had done business with the family for decades. But the flip side of the coin was the one hundred full-time and the sixty-five seasonal employees. The company owed a duty to them as well.

He took the "honest and truthful" approach. "I was open and forthright," Strub says. "I told them: 'I can pay you this much this week but you have to keep the supplies coming. Our forecasts show by this date sixteen weeks out, we're going to be getting caught up.'

"I told them exactly what to expect and delivered," he adds. "We didn't overpromise and underdeliver." The suppliers appreciated his honesty, and all but three supported the company's plan for restructuring.

It taught Strub two lessons. "First, however cold the truth is, however difficult it is, people just want to hear the truth," he says. "Second, people actually *want* to help you."

By the end of 2008, the company was sold to one of its customers, a distributor who wanted manufacturing capability. And Strub was digesting events, writing his resumé and considering his next step. "I had to re-understand myself," he says. He admits it was a hard transition.

"One of the things I learned: never assume your superior knows what you are doing," Strub advises. "In my next career, I'll make sure that the level of communication between my team and my supervisor is very high-level communication."

It isn't just that you want your supervisor to know you are busy; it is more that you want your supervisor to have confidence in you and what you can accomplish. Most important, Strub says, your supervisor will be a mentor to you, if you let him. "Many people want to help you get to where you want to go," he says. "That is true not just in business but also in life."

Strub has since joined NorthBridge Consulting Services based in Cambridge, Ontario, doing tax credit consulting. Only half of the businesses that could be getting money from the federal government's scientific research and experimental development program take advantage of it. The other half don't even know about it, says Strub. It is his job to tell them about it.

"I bring a different perspective," he says. "I am not a salesperson; I am somebody who has gone through the process. I can help them get money." NorthBridge is paid a contingency fee.

"I am rediscovering my self-confidence and sense of self-worth," Strub says. "I did a lot of second-guessing for many years and that can lead to a lot of anxiety. Worry can be a terrible debilitator.

"I have gained a lot of perspective in the past two years," Strub adds. "Having an outside perspective is very important. One thing I didn't gain in the pickle business was perspective. Being able to look at things from different perspectives helps you understand your core business.

"In a lot of ways, selling the company was the worst thing that had ever happened to me," says Strub in retrospect. "In a lot of ways, it was also the best thing that had ever happened to me."

—◁o▷—

Alex Lowy believes no one should be afraid of making mistakes. In fact, the Toronto-based author, consultant and teacher maintains we learn more from our mistakes than we learn from our successes. This learning through adversity is what allows us to surmount obstacles and move forward with our careers and our lives.

"Don't attach too much consequence to failure," Lowy advises. "It is just the price of learning."

Principal and co-founder of the Transcend Strategy Group, Lowy has made a career of understanding organizations that have failed to move forward. A problem solver, he helps organizations and the people in them examine their problems, think strategically and transform themselves. "I am interested in the structure of dilemmas," he says. "If you can name the tension at the core of the dilemma, you can transcend it and evolve beyond it."

Of course, Lowy has had his share of personal successes and failures and it is the resiliency he has learned from the failures that have helped him tackle tough times. His first taste of failure came in Montreal in the early 1970s, when he was working in a post-psychiatric community centre called Dalse House. His insight into the nature of that failure gave him the perspective he needed later in life, especially in 2001 when he faced a situation that had more extensive and personal ramifications.

Rosemary was a schizophrenic who also suffered from bipolar disorder. After being institutionalized for ten years, she came to the centre. Staff was optimistic that with care and appropriate housing arrangements, Rosemary could break the cycle of recidivism and live a non-institution-alized life. It all came off the rails one night when Rosemary decided to jump off a wall in an unsuccessful suicide attempt. She sustained a serious back injury leaving her hospitalized in a body cast. She took to crying and speaking in gibberish whenever anyone was in her room.

Lowy, who had been working closely with Rosemary, went to see her. He couldn't help but notice that it was only when the psychiatrists and social workers came into the room, that Rosemary did most of her crying and odd talking.

'Rosemary, what are you doing?" he recalls asking her when they were alone. "If you keep doing this, they're going to lock you up again."

"I know," Rosemary replied. "But I have to go back in for a while. I really need a rest."

"I was young and idealistic," says Lowy, who admits he was upset and deeply disappointed by Rosemary's setback. "I really believed I could change the world. But Rosemary taught me there are limits to what I — personally — can do. I have a big appetite for taking on challenges. But I learned then that I have to respect others' limits."

Not long after that, Lowy went back to school, and lost contact with Rosemary. He first completed a social sciences degree at Concordia University in Montreal, then a Master of Environmental Studies at York University in Toronto in 1979.

But the lesson stuck with him, and respect for others' limits, both individuals' and organizations', became a cornerstone of his approach to problem solving.

In 1993, after ten years as head of training and development at the City of Toronto, and three years at Shell Canada as an "organization effectiveness advisor," he met his two future business partners while helping solve a crisis at his son's nursery school. Don Tapscott, David Ticoll and Lowy launched new media think-tank, the Alliance for Converging Technologies.

It was a heady time as Lowy and his colleagues researched, conjectured, wrote and consulted on the impact of technology and, Lowy's specialty, its strategic implications for organizations. It was pre-world wide web, and the Alliance was tapping the future for its blue-chip clients. By 2000, the firm employed sixty-five people.

In early 2001, at the top of the dot.com boom, the Alliance (by then re-named Digital 4Sight) was sold to Itemus Inc., a publicly traded company that was fashioning itself as an aggregator of tech companies. Digital 4Sight was to be the strategic engine of the companies Itemus was assembling. The partners received 10% of the purchase price in cash and 90% in shares of the purchaser.

"For a *very* short period," says Lowy, "I was extremely wealthy."

Unfortunately, it didn't last long. Four months later, Itemus went bankrupt. As the share price plummeted, Lowy was left with a big chunk of nothing. "You work hard for ten years and think you have amassed this body of work, and money, and you can focus on other stuff," Lowy says. "It changed in a heartbeat."

Digital 4Sight was the last of the Itemus companies to go bankrupt. Lowy, Tapscott and Ticoll engineered a process whereby they made an offer to the trustee and bought the company back with the support of 51%-partner CGI Group Inc. They then set about the long, tough process of restoring the company to health.

"It is exhausting going through a bankruptcy," recalls Lowy, "the emotional journey of that, the anger of people involved, the expectations of creditors and suppliers."

But it was when dealing with that emotional upheaval and intellectual grind that he tapped into what he had learned in his days working at the post-psychiatric centre. Those accumulated experiences helped him to "roll with the punches."

"All the money was gone and there was an amazing amount of repair work to do," he says, "but the world didn't end. I woke up the next morning — and I still had all my limbs, my senses, and my health."

Once the outlook for Digital 4Sight stabilized, Lowy took a leave of absence, for some "rest and renewal." He set three goals for this period: to play jazz piano; to build a sixteen-foot-square log cabin on a property he and his wife owned; and, to write a book. His piano playing didn't improve as much as he had hoped, although his bass playing did; the cabin was built; and, in 2004, with Phil Hood he published *The Power of the 2 x 2 Matrix*. Lowy and Hood established the Transcend Strategy Group that same year.

"A big part of my work these days is organizational development," Lowy says, "helping companies come to grips with change and the challenges they're facing."

He works with companies large and small, with community groups and not-for-profit organizations. He has developed a strong sense of the mistakes that keep organizations locked in patterns of unproductive behaviour, preventing them from performing at a high level. "When companies become ineffective, it is often because of the disconnects — the misalignment of values and goals with behaviour and practices," he says. "Everybody wants to have a connection between what they are doing with their time and what they value."

Lowy also teaches courses in critical thinking and strategic problem solving at several universities across Canada and internationally. It was while he was developing the framework for these courses that he wrote his most recent book, *No Problem*. He has authored four books in total, including *Digital Capital: Harnessing the Power of Business Webs* in 2000 with former partners Tapscott and Ticoll.

"Staying with things that are hard teaches you a lesson about surviving," Lowy concludes. "We might not choose tough experiences and failure as our teacher, but the learnings that result from them are deep and valuable and trigger real growth and development."

LEARNED SO FAR

- People want to hear the truth.
- People want to help you, in business and in life.
- Don't attach too much consequence to failure; it is just the price of learning.
- Respect others' limits.

CHAPTER EIGHTEEN

Building consensus:
How David Estok
and Rob MacIsaac
learned to resolve conflict

*"The best moments in leadership are when you are able to articulate a
cause in a way in which people will buy in and work toward that cause."*

— ROB MACISAAC

Anyone who has been able to avoid conflict in his or her work or
personal life is leading a charmed life indeed. Inevitably, we run into
a situation that requires all the skill we have to resolve the conflict and
build consensus. Early in his career David Estok found himself in a job
that was rife with conflict. The lessons he learned there have held him in
good stead as he has progressed through life.

For Rob MacIsaac, it is a different story. He chose politics, a hotbed of
dissent, and tackled hot-button issues that challenged his ability to work
collaboratively. But he did it and he counts himself blessed. "It has been an
exciting career," he says. "It has been meaningful, enjoyable and rewarding."

◄o►

David Estok has spent the better part of twenty-five years working in journalism and communications. He has had his share of challenges — as a journalist covering the steel and automotive industry for the *Financial Post* newspaper, developing courses in newsroom management at University of Western Ontario and, most recently, trying to change newsroom culture at the *Hamilton Spectator*, a major daily newspaper in Hamilton, Ontario.

But when he talks about his greatest challenge, the experience that changed how he approached his work ever afterward, he talks about his role as communications director at the newly created Workplace Health and Safety Agency (WHSA) in Toronto in the early 1990s.

The agency was a bipartite labour/management organization created by the Ontario government in 1990. Its goal was admirable, to reduce the number of accidents and deaths in Ontario workplaces, but, from its start, it was destined to engender conflict. It had joint CEOs — one from labour, one from management — which pitted traditional adversaries against each other. And workplace safety itself was controversial. It was a prescription for disaster.

"I learned a lot about managing conflict," says Estok, "and the ability to work collaboratively and build consensus."

He stayed at WHSA for four years, but what he learned has lasted him a lifetime. As Estok's career progressed, and concepts such as "shared authority" and "empowering" employees gained credence in business-management circle, the skills learned at WHSA became even more important. "Try doing that if you don't know how to manage conflict," he says. "It's impossible."

Estok was certainly familiar with conflict. He had been a reporter at the *Hamilton Spectator* in the mid-1980s, when he was recruited to the *Financial Post* in 1987. So, he knew first-hand that newsrooms and journalists thrive on conflict. In fact, a good news story hinges on conflict, and a reporter's ability to deliver that story depends on his or her ability to burrow into the centre of that conflict. It takes resolve to be a good reporter — and Estok was a good reporter.

So, when he went to WHSA as communications director, he found himself without the tools he needed to do his job. "I was a young person struggling to do work I had never done before," he says. "I was a newspaper person.

"Conflict in a corporate environment is very destructive," Estok adds, "for the person and for the company. It is soul-destroying; it makes it impossible to do work that you feel good about."

The first thing Estok learned: have empathy. And you can't do that without developing your listening skills. "Openly listen," he advises, "without judging."

When a co-worker categorically disagrees or refuses to see another's point of view, Estok recommends that — rather than reacting — you ask yourself: "Why is this person saying this? What is he (or she) thinking? What can I understand about this person from his (or her) reaction?"

The second lesson revolves around criticism. "It is normal to be defensive when you are given negative feedback," Estok says, "No matter how good you are at your job, how positive you feel about it, your first reaction is to be defensive."

His learned response: thank the person for the feedback, then probe. Ask the questions that will unlock the meaning of the comments.

Third, Estok recommends "filtering" — going away and thinking about it. What filters through might be less contentious than you thought.

In 2007, Estok was lured back into journalism. While at Western as associate vice president of communications and public affairs, he had created and taught a course on newsroom management in the university's journalism program. So when he took the call to become editor-in-chief of the *Hamilton Spectator*, he saw it as an opportunity to put theory into practice.

"I was coming into the *Spectator* at a time of tremendous change in the industry," Estok says. "I had been watching it carefully for ten years. I wanted to try out some of the ideas I had taught."

Newspapers are traditionally hierarchical. The editor-in-chief calls the shots and his or her editors go away and execute. It is expedient and straightforward. Estok wanted to try something different, something he felt was in keeping with the times. As editor-in-chief, he wanted to set the direction of and the vision for the news coverage. The day-to-day decision-making would be pushed down to section editors, making it a more collaborative effort.

"Newsrooms are getting smaller," he explains. There are fewer reporters and fewer editors. "Authority needs to get pushed down."

Did it work? Estok admits it is hard to change newsroom culture. It was worth the try. But when he got a call from a former boss in March 2010 to join him at SickKids Foundation in Toronto as vice president of communications, he made the move.

As for WHSA, his experience there was invaluable, he says: "For me to learn the other side of my personality was so valuable."

—◦—

Rob MacIsaac has made a career of building consensus and getting people to act collaboratively. He has worked at the local, regional and provincial levels of government helping develop policies that allow those levels of government to work together on issues that affect all three.

When he says it was "hugely challenging," there is not a trace of regret in his voice.

"The best moments in leadership," he says, "are when you are able to articulate a cause in a way in which people will buy in and work toward that cause."

A lawyer by profession, MacIsaac entered city politics in 1991, two years after he was called to the bar. At the urging of an old friend, he ran for city council in Burlington, a booming city in Ontario's Golden Horseshoe. Although he had always professed an interest in life in public service, when it did happen, he admits it felt more like happenstance than design.

"But once I was in," MacIsaac adds, "it was like eating a bag of potato chips: you can't stop until you eat the whole thing."

He spent six years as a councillor, then nine years as mayor of Burlington. It was in that period, from 1997 to 2006, when he became interested in issues that had a local impact but which, from a policy perspective, originated at a regional or even provincial level, such as transportation and highways, urban sprawl and agriculture.

"The longer I worked as mayor, the more interested I became in issues that had a regional context," MacIsaac says. "I am a firm believer in local government, but some issues need to be dealt with at a regional level."

During his time as Burlington's mayor, MacIsaac was on the Ontario government's Smart Growth Panel which tackled the issue of urban sprawl, transportation and land use in the various regions of Ontario. He served as chairman of the strategic planning sub-panel of the Central Ontario Smart Growth Panel. The panel submitted its final report in 2003.

In 2004, MacIsaac chaired Ontario's thirteen-member Greenbelt Task Force, which was tasked with finding a way to protect green space and contain urban sprawl in the Golden Horseshoe. The 2006 Greenbelt Act protects 1.8 million acres of sensitive land from development.

These were contentious issues, and many viewpoints were represented, but MacIsaac enjoyed every minute of it. "In my nine years as mayor," he says, "there was never a Sunday night when I didn't feel like starting work Monday morning."

In 2006, MacIsaac was offered the full-time position of chairman of Metrolinx, a crown agency that was established to develop a transportation plan for the Golden Horseshoe. "It was an extraordinarily difficult decision to leave the mayor's job," he says. "I loved what I was doing. But transportation was the third leg of the stool. It linked smart growth and green space together."

As chairman, MacIsaac was responsible for the start up of Metrolinx and the development of a plan that encompassed the transportation needs of the Greater Toronto and Hamilton area. The plan, entitled *The Big Move: Transforming Transportation in the Greater Toronto and Hamilton Area,* was adopted in November 2008. "We were able to grow Metrolinx from one employee to a combined Metrolinx-GO Transit with two thousand employees," he says. "We got it off to a strong start."

The Smart Growth Panel, the Greenbelt Task Force and Metrolinx were all challenging exercises that demanded time and creativity. "There was an extraordinary diversity of interests," MacIsaac says. "We needed to find solutions that represented the common good."

The way to do that, he adds, was to get everyone to put aside their local interests and share in a vision of a vibrant city, region and province. "We needed to find a way to drive toward that vision," MacIsaac says.

As leader it was his job to articulate that vision and it was a role with which MacIsaac was increasingly comfortable. "Confidence is an important part of success in leadership. Confidence helps you to do more and more."

MacIsaac suffered what he calls the "inverse of confidence" when, as a twenty-six-year-old, he dove into a lake and broke his neck. "It put me in touch with my own mortality," he says, an unlikely spot for a young man. "It shook my confidence. It took me a while to get it back."

But it had one repercussion that MacIsaac hadn't foreseen. "It gave me the confidence that if I fail, it is not going to be the end of the world," he says. "You pick yourself up and start over again."

In February 2009, just as he was ready to "declare victory" at Metrolinx, MacIsaac was offered the presidency of Mohawk College, a community college in Hamilton. "It came at a good time," he says. "It took me off in an entirely new direction. The most interesting and rewarding times are when I put myself into a place that is uncomfortable."

And Mohawk isn't really so different from his past experiences. "It is a lot about people," he says, "and getting them to pull together to work toward a common vision."

LEARNED SO FAR

- Develop your listening skills.
- Don't be defensive when faced with negative feedback.
- Go away and think about it.
- Clearly articulate the vision if you expect people to work for a common cause.

CHAPTER NINETEEN

Leading the way: How Stephen Smith, Mandeep Malik and Judith Hills show leadership

"In a world where there is no such thing as sustainable competitive advantage, Leaders must Lead!"

— JOHN O. BURDETT

What makes a person a leader is very hard to define. Is it, as suggested by Rob MacIsaac in the previous chapter, the ability to articulate a vision in such a way that people are willing to put aside their personal interests for the common good? Or is it defined by the relationship of the leader to the people he or she is leading, as expressed by Stephen Smith below?

But leadership can also be defined in terms of teaching and inspiring the next generation of leaders in their thinking, as Mandeep Malik has done. And what about changing the way the public thinks about an issue such as mental illness? If you are changing public perception, as Judith Hills has done, isn't that, too, leadership?

"The only difference between any two companies, in the long run, is their leadership teams," says Smith. "The good leaders will lead their companies to success." That works outside the corporate environment, too.

With almost thirty years' experience in the airline industry, Stephen Smith has picked up more than a few diplomas from the School of Hard Knocks. And as an unpaid executive-in-residence at the DeGroote School of Business at McMaster University in Hamilton, Ontario, and the Ivey School of Business at University of Western Ontario in London, Ontario, he is happy to share what he has learned.

A proven leader, Smith has much to say on the nature of leadership and what makes a leader. But he hasn't always been so knowledgeable. Although he always liked the idea of being out in front, early in his career he didn't really understand leading, and the relationship of the leader to the people he or she leads. "When I was twenty-five," he confides, "I was brash and going for the top as quickly as I could — and I was climbing on people."

Smith learned, but it was knowledge gained at a cost — to him and to other people.

A native of Burlington, Ontario, Smith graduated from the University of Waterloo with a Bachelor of Mathematics in 1976. In 1979 he graduated top second in his Master of Business Administration class at McMaster, which gave him his pick of three great job opportunities: Bell Canada, Xerox Corp. and Air Canada.

"All three positions were similar," he recalls. "So, I said: 'Well, okay, what do I want to do in my free time? Do I want to make free phone calls, do I want to Xerox my hand or do I want to fly for free?' So, I went into aviation. I was at Air Canada three different times during my career for a total of eighteen years."

Smith has seen a plethora of change in his time in aviation management. He entered the business when it was government-controlled and fares and schedules were all set by Ottawa. All that changed with deregulation in 1987. Domestic travel has since become a "free for all," Smith says. Competition rules the industry and flyers are wooed with promises of service, frequent flyer points and discounted fares. With the exception of safety regulations, Canada's airlines are as unfettered as any other business when it comes to attracting and serving passengers.

"Aviation doesn't just change," says Smith, "it changes daily."

Smith participated in a lot of those changes. He was part of the team that brought in Air Canada's frequent flyer program, Aeroplan, and he engineered the integration of Air Canada and its "connector" carriers, now known as Jazz. He was also at Air Canada in 2003, when the airline filed for bankruptcy protection under the Canadian Companies' Creditor Arrangement Act.

"I was then president of ZIP, which was Air Canada's low-fare airline in Western Canada," Smith recalls. "I had a team of people who were saying 'What about us? What happens to us?'"

Fortunately, Smith had learned a thing or two about leadership by that time. He had left Air Canada in 1988 to be the president of Air Toronto, an Air Canada connector airline flying from Toronto into the U.S. After Air Toronto's parent company went into receivership, Air Toronto was sold to Canadian Regional Airlines. Smith returned to Air Canada and, in 1995, became president of its regional subsidiary Air Ontario. He had also done an eighteen-month stint as president and CEO at competitor WestJet, returning once again to Air Canada in 2001.

One of his most painful lessons was learned at Air Ontario, when, during a speech to the management team, he made some less than flattering remarks about the organization's monthly newsletter and the manager of communications who was responsible for it. "I tended to be an off-the-cuff individual," Smith admits. "I wasn't throwing a bomb at her intentionally; it was meant to be a humourous comment — and it was devastating to her.

"From that I learned a number of things," he continues. "One, when you're at the top of the heap, the most important meeting or encounter employees can have that week, that month, that year, will be with you. Two, every-thing you say gets dissected and analyzed. So, you have to be very careful what you say. And I hadn't taken the time to find out the whole story. Third, wait until you know the whole story, and never — intentionally or unintentionally — ridicule someone. People are looking up to you, they're leaning on you. So, what you do and say defines the company."

Smith had also had the good fortune to work with a boss who taught him how to curb his directness and his tendency to barge right in. "I was very task-oriented and he was instrumental in making me realize that: a) there are people out there; and b) there's a way of dealing with those people to get what you want."

So, by the time Air Canada was in bankruptcy protection and ZIP's future was uncertain, Smith had developed some sensitivity to his colleagues and their concerns. He chose to treat them with respect and honesty, recognizing they had genuine reason for concern. As soon as he knew something, they knew it, too.

"I realized that I needed to set the tenor of how we were going to deal with this," he says. "Everybody recognized that there are certain things you can't control, but what you can control is the job you've been given. If you do that to the absolute best of your ability, then you'll know that you've done everything you could. If the decision was to shut us down, we would know that we did everything we could to make us a success.

"It's the best thing to do," Smith maintains, "because it gives your work meaning."

Eight months after Air Canada filed for bankruptcy protection, ZIP was shut down. Smith stayed on with Air Canada as the airline emerged from bankruptcy as senior vice president, customer experience, until 2005.

Now that Smith is in an academic environment, he has turned his critical eye to what MBA students are being taught. There is not enough emphasis on "soft" skills, such as sales skills, he maintains. "It's the one thing that should be taught," he says. "Every day of your management career, you'll be selling — an idea, a product, yourself, your company. Selling isn't about telling people stuff; it's about listening and establishing relationships."

And, of course, the other soft skill schools should be teaching is leadership. It is the quality that sets people apart; leadership skills are the reason people get promotions, says Smith: "It's your ability to get along with people, your ability to work with people and, most important, your ability to lead people."

Read books on leadership, he recommends, study leadership, find a mentor. "Leadership is like being a father or a husband or a coach," Smith concludes, "you can always get better. I would like to be a better leader; I would like to continue improving. In five or ten years, I just hope that I'm an even better leader than what I am now."

◄○►

Mandeep Malik is a leader of a different sort. He is not leading a corporate entity, but, as assistant professor of Strategic Market Leadership and Health Services Management at the DeGroote School of Business, he is showing the way to corporate Canada's future leaders.

His goal, he says, is to foster motivated learners: "I am embedding lifelong learning, citizenship, leadership and social responsibility behaviours that will serve my students well for years to come. Seeing my students grow and prosper years later warms my heart and, somewhere inside, I am achieving my dreams through them."

Malik is particularly well-equipped to nurture his students. In 1995, he faced a life-changing decision that could have been adverse to his career. But he weighed the costs and benefits and accepted the challenge. Only later did he realize he had seriously underestimated the rewards of his decision, and the impact it would have on his career as an educator.

In 1995, Malik was in a senior management position with a division of NIIT Ltd., a fast-growing training and performance coaching company based in New Delhi, India. His career was on an upward trajectory with responsibilities, financial rewards and influence increasing with almost every quarter. The next "C-level" job was just around the corner.

His wife Arinder, too, was enjoying success in her career as a specialist physician. And their family was growing; their first child was two and a half years old and a second child was on the way. "We were both enjoying fairly successful careers," says Malik. "We had our families around us and much to look forward to."

The spanner in the works occurred when Arinder was one of a handful of candidates selected to pursue a prized Clinical Fellowship in Sydney, Australia. "I had to make a choice between my growth and my wife's growth," Malik says. "I had to choose to uproot us and lose the benefit of family; I had to decide if the opportunities of the developed world were better for my kids than the easy access to grandparents."

But in the end, it was essentially an easy decision. "What made it easy was the understanding of where my priorities lay," he explains, "and what was important to *us*."

Malik decided to take a one-year paternity leave and be a stay-at-home dad so his wife could pursue her dream. "My friends were stunned, my employer horrified," he recalls, "even my mother was a little baffled."

He considers his mother a strong role model, and he has always admired her strength of character, her courage to choose "the right path, not the easy path."

So, he moved his family to Sydney and assumed the roles of homemaker and child-care provider. "There was no compromise of ego involved," he says, "just the thought of what family meant."

Although he admits to having a lot to learn, it worked. The paternity leave extended to two years and morphed into a new life. In 1997-1999, he did his MBA at the University of Canberra in Australia, collaborating with academics, policy makers and business leaders to develop his dissertation on business education. In June 1999, he and his family moved to Hamilton, so he could take up residence as assistant professor at McMaster.

"The time I spent nurturing and being with our children in their formative years was the reward I had not anticipated," Malik says. "Upon reflection, that reward almost trivializes the challenge I faced in 1995. To see them grow, mature and become their own persons with strong family values is a true blessing."

That attitude has direct bearing on his role as an educator, in which he participates in the growth and development of a new generation of business leaders. A strong believer in the capabilities and capacity of his students, Malik has become a master of developing experiential learning programs, including *Canada's Next Top Ad Executive, Synergy,* Marketing & Retail Sales *Apprentice, High School Business Heroes, Focus 2040* and *Let's Do Business.*

"I engender humility in learning by expressing humility," he says, "and standing beside my students to see issues from their point of view and partner in the process of problem solving. It is my firm belief that students must come up with the solutions and know that they did, *that they can.*"

Malik often reflects on what he left behind and stays in touch with former colleagues. But he has no regrets; he knows he chose the right path, not the easy path. "If you want to be a teacher," he admonishes, "know that you must love learning. Enjoy debate. Thrive on disagreement. Have the courage to lose your ego. Know that to think, to rethink and then question your very own thought process is to grow."

"Above all," Malik says, "remember that you will not be recognized in life for what you have accumulated but what you have spread. Have the courage to be honest, truthful and fully committed to all."

—◦—

Judith Hills admits her first love is teaching, even though she left the classroom behind almost forty years ago. But over the course of her twenty-eight-year career in the not-for-profit sector in Toronto, the organizations with which she has worked have changed the way people think about their physical and mental health. You could say Hills has become an educator in a classroom without walls, a leader of public perception.

By writing educational material, implementing public awareness programs, corralling volunteers and cajoling donors, Hills has tackled issues such as parenting skills, children's stress, workplace stress and work/life balance, and the stigma surrounding mental illness. She has done it with grace, conviction and dedication.

"Passion for what you are doing is so critical," Hills says. "In the not-for-profit sector, you have to have a bit of the entrepreneurial spirit. There just aren't the resources. You have to be ready to pick it up and do it."

Hills has certainly done just that. A graduate of McMaster University in chemistry in 1963, she started teaching high-school mathematics, sciences, and physical health and education when she was twenty. Those were the days when Ontario needed teachers and young graduates earned their teaching certificates at summer school. Hills taught high school for seven years, but when her two boys were born, she stayed at home for ten years. She kept her hand in, teaching summer courses for teachers at the University of Toronto's Faculty of Education.

When it came time to re-enter the workforce full-time, however, teaching jobs had evaporated. An active volunteer writing education materials for the Canadian Cancer Society while she was at home, she found a job as program coordinator at the Lung Association. She stayed sixteen years and her last job was executive director for Toronto and York Region.

"While I was there, it occurred to me how very fortunate I was," Hills says. "I am delighted there were no teaching jobs. So many other opportunities were the result of that change."

One such opportunity came in 1998, when Hills was recruited by the Canadian Psychiatric Research Foundation (CPRF) as executive director. It was a very small charity — with only two staff — whose purpose was fundraising. "It was a wonderful move," she says. "There was an incredible board of directors, all focused on the single task of raising money for research for mental health and addiction. I learned a tremendous amount from them."

Although Hills had experience in not-for-profit, she didn't have business experience, but she learned that in spades from her board, which was made up of bank presidents and CEOs from major corporations. "They taught me how to be tougher," she says.

She needed to get tougher, she admits, because when it comes to fundraising, mental health is a hard sell. "There is a stigma attached to it," Hills says. "There is a lot of fear attached to mental illness."

During her eight years at CPRF, the organization set out to change those perceptions. In the early days of her tenure it was as straightforward as developing a communications plan to explain what the CPRF did and tell the public how it could help. But while it may have been straightforward, it wasn't simple. "In a not-for-profit, you don't just pick up the phone and call a consultant," says Hills. "There aren't the resources."

Such projects come to fruition through the efforts of volunteers. For example, her neighbour volunteered her son, a website designer, to build CPRF a website. A friend was recruited to develop a newsletter. Another group of volunteers wrote education and information pieces. Hills and her board members found corporate partners to back specific projects.

Later, the new chair of the CPRF, Kevin McNeil, decided it was time to launch a campaign battling the social stigma associated with having a mental illness. They set about finding money to fund the campaign. They raised $1 million but in the end it was volunteers that did the heavy lifting. Staff of advertising agency Vickers and Benson Arnold Worldwide donated their time to the award-winning print, TV and radio campaign, as did the actors. A long list of newspapers and magazines donated space for the print campaign; radio and TV stations in Canada and the U.S. made air time available.

"It was a hard-hitting campaign," says Hills. For example, the TV commercial showed a man in a suit getting hit by a car. Bystanders rush over to the immobile figure in the middle of the road, but when they see no obvious signs of injury, they walk away saying, "He probably just doesn't want to go to work." The campaign ran with the tag line "Imagine if we treated everyone like we treat the mentally ill."

In April 2006, Hills decided the CPRF needed someone to take the organization to "the next level" and she needed a rest. She retired. "We were working sixty hours a week," she says. "There were only two of us."

Her "retirement" lasted a week. The Psychology Foundation Canada (PFC) needed an executive director and she jumped at it. "It was an opportunity to become more involved with actual programs on the prevention side of things," Hills says. "And by then, I had the background that could help the PFC realize its dream."

The mission of the PFC is to share sound psychological knowledge to better people's lives, and it has focused on children and families. A large part of the job is fundraising — "We still need money for everything," says Hills — but that money gets spent on developing programming, such as the *Parenting for Life* series of booklets. *The Kids Have Stress, Too* program, which is designed to help parents and caregivers understand childhood stress, started at a pre-school level and now has classroom versions that extend right up to eighth grade. The goal is to embed the program in early childhood education training.

"We want children to learn the tools for handling stress early on," says Hills. "Then they can use them their whole lives."

The PFC has turned its attention to dealing with stress in newcomer families with the Diversity Action Scarborough project. Once the program is evaluated, it will be rolled out across the country. Workplace mental health is another program that is already being rolled out across the country in a series of lunch and learns.

It was meant to be a three-days-a-week job. That makes Hills laugh. "If you are not there, you miss opportunities," she says. "You can't afford to miss opportunities. There are 400,000 not-for-profits looking for money, resources and volunteers."

In fact, Hills says, her biggest challenge is knowing when to say "No."

"Part of the job is helping other people realize their dreams," she says. "The volunteers have wonderful ideas, but we can't operationalize them all. The danger is taking on too much."

Hills didn't start out to have a career in the not-for-profit sector. "In fact," she says ruefully, "women of my age didn't have career plans." Yet, there is no mistaking what she has accomplished in her career.

"I always choose the tough path," she admits, "I am a person who likes challenges — and I want to make a difference."

LEARNED SO FAR

- Be very careful what you say.
- Never — intentionally or unintentionally — ridicule someone.
- There are certain things you can't control, but what you can control is the job you've been given to do.
- Enjoy debate. Thrive on disagreement. Have the courage to lose your ego. Know that to think, to rethink and then question your very own thought process is to grow.
- Passion for what you are doing is critical.

Life is full
of surprises

Yogi Berra's wife, Carmen, once asked her husband: "Yogi, you are from St. Louis, we live in New Jersey, and you played ball in New York. If you go before I do, where would you like me to have you buried?"

Yogi replied, "Surprise me."

Life is full of surprises, as our fifty "graduates" of the School of Hard Knocks have demonstrated. They have told us their stories of life-changing events that strengthened their resolve, taught them to roll with the punches and propelled them forward. Although they come from different backgrounds and different walks of life, the lessons the fifty learned aren't so different. There are a number of common themes, proving once again, that in our differences lie our commonalities.

So what did we learn?

- Don't let the fear of making a mistake keep you from living life to the fullest. As Alex Lowy says, mistakes are the price you pay for learning.

Or if you take Susan Caldwell's approach, it is only a mistake if you can't recover from it. So, it isn't really a mistake if you learn from it.

This is not permission to do foolish things, but rather an admonition to see mistakes as mere bumps in the road. And the more you learn from your mistakes, the easier it gets. Experience builds perspective. So, when you hit that big pothole, two things happen: thanks to the perspective you have gained, you see it for what it is and take it in stride; and, second, you have built some coping mechanisms. As Lowy likes to say, "It's not the end of the world."

- Expect the unexpected. Life can be hard, full of sharp corners and steep hills. It's fine to plan, but, as Major Alex Ruff points out, be ready to adjust your plan because some parts of the plan will work, some won't. Be flexible and adaptable, he advises. Roll with the punches. If you can't adopt, you'll get stuck in the past.

Galit Solomon provides a powerful example of that. Sexually abused as a twelve-year-old, she came to realize she had to let go of the past and move on. She is doing that by helping others who have had the same tragic experience as herself. That leads to the next lesson.

- People want to help one another. As Denise Bellamy discovered when her husband was dying of cancer, you don't need to go through life's tragedies alone. People want to help. People write books they hope will help, they volunteer at centres such as Wellspring. And when Bellamy joined grief groups, she found she, too, could help — that there were people who were worse off than she was and she could lend them her strength.

Arthur Sutcliffe had the same experience when he turned to Alcoholics Anonymous to battle his addiction. He is now helping others battle addiction — and in that is his salvation.

It isn't any different at a business level, as Arnie Strub discovered. When he was in the throes of recapitalizing the family business, he found support in an unlikely place, his suppliers. They wanted to help. Strub sees that now as a life lesson. Whatever you are doing, people want to help you to be the best you can be.

So, don't be afraid to ask for help. People like to give back. It all comes around.

- Good people have good values. But more important, they live by those values. In fact, in many cases, life is an exploration of just how to do that.

  Take Terry Jacks, for example. And Andy Creeggan. Both are talented musicians with a passion for making music. Naturally enough, that led them into the music business. But over time, they came to realize it wasn't in tune with their values. So, they each adapted their life style to align with their values.

  There are many examples in *What I Have Learned So Far* of people making unusual or unpopular choices in order to be true to their values. Think Scott Bowman and how his belief in the power of self-disciple and personal responsibility materialized in a military college. Or Justin Cooper and how his faith in Christ found expression leading a Christian university.

  As Maureen Jensen says so clearly, "Never compromise your ethics — listen to your inner voice and it will guide you."

- Tell the truth; be open and honest. This is another lesson Arnie Strub learned in difficult circumstances. And he learned it well. When the fat hit the fire, he told the truth. He didn't overpromise and underdeliver. "However cold the truth is, however difficult it is," he says, "people just want to hear the truth."

- Learn the language of consensus and working collaboratively. From sports to business to politics, it is important to find a way to work together. Early in his career, David Estok found himself in a job grounded in conflict. He had to learn to temper his own "dukes up" approach, hold his own ego in check and listen, really listen to what the person was saying — as well as what he or she wasn't saying.

  Olympic athlete Marnie McBean had a similar epiphany. She had to accept that not everyone approached sport and competition the same way as she did. She had to make room in her life for differences in approach. Like Estok, she had to set her ego aside; she learned to communicate, to talk *to* people and not *at* people.

  David Crombie and Rob MacIsaac wouldn't have survived in politics if they hadn't been able to build consensus. "You have to listen," Crombie says, "because most people don't want to fight to the death; most people want to fight to some kind of solution."

- Take leadership; stand up for what you believe in. It may be easier, when you hit an obstacle in your path, just to take a detour. That way you avoid confrontation, and everybody's happy. But Yaser Haddara and Rob Girouard would debate that. In very different circumstances, they stood up for what they believed in. Haddara's stand won him tenure at his university; Girouard's took him to Afghanistan with the Canadian Forces, even after his dad was killed there. If he turned tail and ran, he says, it was acknowledging defeat. And Girouard is no loser.

- We are all teachers and salespeople. Stephen Smith is right when he says that every day, every minute of your career (and life, we might add) you'll be selling — your products, your company, your ideas, yourself. "Selling isn't about telling people stuff," he says. "It's about listening and establishing relationships."

  The same goes for teaching. Whether it is in the classroom, or in the workplace or at home, we are always doing our best to help and teach others. McMaster University professor Mandeep Malik has a wonderful prescription for teaching that can be applied to life. "Know that you must love learning," he says. "Enjoy debate. Thrive on disagreement. Have the courage to lose your ego. Know that to think, to rethink and then question your very own thought process is to grow."

- Do what you love. It has worked for Jim Letwin and Susan Caldwell. Judith Hills certainly feels that way about her work in the not-for-profit sector. Mario Lechowski feels that way about teaching boxing. In fact, it would be hard to find any of the fifty that didn't place a high priority on doing something you love. It may take a while to find out what you really love doing, but that's okay: life is a work in progress.

We could go on. There are many other lessons. We just picked the low-hanging fruit. But what we have wanted to show is that most crises have solutions; what matters is your ability to recognize the solution and implement it.

—◦—

In Frigyes Karinthy's 1929 short story, *Chains*, the Hungarian writer suggested that anyone in the world could be connected to anyone else through a chain of no more than five intermediaries. The life stories that have been shared here have been found through the randomness of personal connection, yet the lessons are universal. A lesson learned in Afghanistan can be applied in Burlington. The situations may change but the solutions remain the same.

Leadership comes from connection; connection comes from authenticity. Authenticity comes from being comfortable in your own skin; being comfortable in your own skin comes from being vulnerable. We have heard from authentic people who, today, are comfortable in their own skins. Hopefully, their journeys will make your way a little smoother.

RESOURCES LIST

Perhaps the strategies suggested by the fifty individuals profiled in this book will lead you further in your search for solutions. The individuals to whom we spoke suggested some of the resources listed here, but the list is by no means exhaustive. If you need further assistance, contact the authors at LearnedSoFar@alemid.com

Afghanistan Issues

Kandahar Tour: The Turning Point in Canada's Afghan Mission, written by Drs. Lee Windsor, David Charters and David Wilson and published by the Gregg Centre for the Study of War and Society at the University of New Brunswick (2008), delineates Canadian operations in Afghanistan. *www.unb.ca/fredericton/arts/centres/gregg*

Alcoholism and Drug Addiction

Alcoholics Anonymous supports individuals in their struggle to overcome alcoholism. *www.aa.org*

Cocaine Anonymous works with individuals looking to overcome their addiction. *www.ca.org*

Child Abuse

Boost Child Abuse Prevention & Intervention works to eliminate abuse and violence in the lives of children, adolescents and their families. *www.boostforkids.org*

Project Butterflies, operated by Galit Solomon, provides resources and contacts. *www.projectbutterflies.org*

Entrepreneurs

The mandate of the Canadian Federation of Independent Business is supporting, advising and saving money for Canadian entrepreneurs. *www.cfib-fcei.ca*

The Government of Canada has a program entitled the Scientific Research and Experimental Development Tax Incentive program which provides tax incentives to businesses which pay for development and research. *www.cra-arc.gc.ca/sred/*

Employment Help

The federal government provides several sites with job-hunting information and tools including *www.workingincanada.gc.ca* and *www.hrsdc-drhc.gc.ca*

Financial Education

The Knowledge Bureau is a private post-secondary educational institute and publisher providing continuing education mainly in tax and wealth-management for the financial services industry. *www.knowledgebureau.com*

The Toronto Stock Exchange and its parent, the TMX Group, have a website that provides consumers trading and statistical information about the markets, market research and personal financial knowledge. *www.TMXmoney.com*

Financial Planning and Debt Assistance

There are a number of website that will connect a consumer to a qualified financial advisor:

- Advocis, the Financial Planners Association of Canada. *www.advocis.ca*

- The Canadian Institute of Financial Planners. *www.cifps.ca*

- The Independent Financial Brokers of Canada. *www.iabc.ca*

- The Institute of Advanced Financial Planner. *www.iafp.ca*

The Certified General Accountants Association of Canada issued a report in May 2010, which tracks increases in household debt, entitled *Where Is the Money Now: The State of Canadian Household Debt as Conditions for Economic Recovery Emerge.* The report can be found at *www.cga-canada.org/en-ca/ ResearchAndAdvocacy/AreasofInterest/DebtandConsumption/Pages/ca_debt_ default.aspx*

Credit Canada assists individuals with debt problems and money management education. *www.creditcanada.com*

The Credit Counselling Society provides financial counselling and training in money management. *www.nomoredebts.org*

The Task Force on Financial Literacy plans to present a report on the financial literacy of Canadians to the Minister of Finance the end of 2010. *www.financialliteracyincanada.com*

Health

The Brain That Changes Itself: Stories of Personal Triumph from the Frontiers of Brain Science written by Dr. Norman Doidge and published by James H. Silberman Books, challenges the belief that the human brain cannot be changed and provides evidence that the brain can, in effect, re-wire itself after being damaged by medical or behavioural disorders. *www.normandoidge.com*

The Heart and Stroke Foundation of Canada provides information on recognizing and coping with strokes and blood pressure problems, as well as other healthy living topics. *www.heartandstroke.ca*

Jill Bolte Taylor got a research opportunity few brain scientists would wish for: she had a massive stroke, and watched as her brain functions — motion, speech, self-awareness — shut down one by one. For a moving yet informative description of what it is like to have a stroke, go to *www.ted. com/talks/lang/eng/jill_bolte_taylor_s_powerful_stroke_of_insight.html*

Wellspring operates a network of centres in various Canadian cities to provide information and support to cancer patients and their families. *www.wellspring.ca*

The Dave Irwin Foundation for Brain Injuries raises money to support research into brain injuries. *www.daveirwinfoundation.org*

The Canadian Psychiatric Research Foundation raises money to research mental illnesses. To see its ad campaign countering the stigma associated with mental illness, go to *cprf.ca.*

The Psychology Foundation of Canada is a not-for-profit organization that develops programming to support children and families. Its materials can be downloaded from its website. *www.psychologyfoundation.org*

Sports

The Government of Alberta maintains a site containing ideas called Healthy Alberta with information on active living, healthy eating, self-esteem through sports and other topics at *http://www.healthyalberta.com.*

Volunteering to Help in Disasters

Humanity First Canada, the Canadian operation of Humanity First International, is a Canada-based international humanitarian relief organization. *www.humanityfirst.ca*

Habitat For Humanity Canada, the Canadian operation of Habitat For Humanity, contributes to the organization's relief efforts in Haiti and other disaster areas. *www.habitat.ca*

Pierspective Entraide Humanitaire holds fundraising activities and collects medical and educational equipment for shipment to Haiti. *www.haitiaide.ca*

UNICEF CANADA, the Canadian operation of UNICEF, raises funds for UNICEF's work with children around the world. *www.unicef.ca*

Index

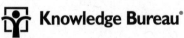